California Natural History Guides: 11

SPRING
WILDFLOWERS

OF THE

SAN FRANCISCO BAY REGION

BY

HELEN K. SHARSMITH

UNIVERSITY OF CALIFORNIA PRESS
BERKELEY, LOS ANGELES, LONDON

ERRATA

Please note there may be an error in page sequence
between pages 69/70, 77/78, 85/86 and 93/94. All
pages are contained in the binding. We apologize
for this printer's error.

UNIVERSITY OF CALIFORNIA PRESS
BERKELEY AND LOS ANGELES, CALIFORNIA

UNIVERSITY OF CALIFORNIA PRESS, LTD.
LONDON, ENGLAND

STANDARD BOOK NUMBER 520-01168-6
LIBRARY OF CONGRESS CATALOG CARD NUMBER: 64-21067
PRINTED IN THE UNITED STATES OF AMERICA

5 6 7 8 9 0

CONTENTS

ACKNOWLEDGMENTS

Permission to use appropriate illustrations from Willis Lynn Jepson's "A Manual of the Flowering Plants of California," "Flora of California," and "Trees, Shrubs and Flowers of the Redwood Region" was granted by the Trustees of the Jepson Herbarium, University of California, and also, for the third title, by the Save-the-Redwoods League. The remainder of the illustrations were drawn mainly by Emily Reid and Charlotte Mentges (the latter also painted the cover-design), while Jean Colton illustrated the plant-terms. A few kodachromes are by G. T. Robbins, from the Jepson Herbarium; most are by Charles Webber from the collections of the California Academy of Sciences, the Sierra Club, the Jepson Herbarium, and the University of California Herbarium. I am appreciative of all the assistance received from these people and institutions and, in addition, from my colleagues.

SAN FRANCISCO BAY REGION

INTRODUCTION

To enjoy using this book, learn its limitations, for to ignore them will lead to frustration. With perhaps a thousand kinds of flowering plants in the San Francisco Bay Region, there are here included as spring wildflowers only about 300 kinds. Obviously many limitations had to be set and, nature lacking sharp boundaries, choices often had to be arbitrary. These are the plants excluded: woody plants (trees and shrubs); introduced weeds; "escaped" garden plants; grasses, rushes, sedges; summer- and fall-blooming wildflowers; spring wildflowers very rare or inconspicuous in our area.

What, then, are wildflowers? With several answers possible, we view them here as native perennial or annual herbs with usually obvious flowers. Perennial herbs have woody underground roots or stems which enable them to live many years, but their aboveground stems are never woody, dying back to the soil each dormant season; annual herbs have *no* woody parts, live but one growing season, and "winter over" by means of seeds. Of wildflowers so defined, we consider here only spring wildflowers, of which a few begin to bloom in January, some in February, most in March, some in April or even May. The great mass of bloom, however, reaches its peak in late March or early April and begins to decline by late April.

The woody plants of the San Francisco Bay Region are to be treated in two books in this series, trees (Metcalf, 1960) and shrubs (not yet published). Other similar books are planned for ferns and weeds. Unfortunately for spring wildflower enthusiasts, many weeds (plants out-of-place) are annual or perennial herbs and hence may be easily confused with native wildflowers. To be sure, weeds, which follow man's transgressions upon the natural scene, are more abundant in disturbed areas, but where in the Bay Region have man's transgressions not been felt? To use this book successfully, you will need to keep an open mind on native plants vs. the excluded weeds.

Where, also, to draw the line between spring wildflowers and the excluded summer wildflowers? There are no sharp breaks in the blooming schedule and on the heels of late spring wildflowers (April and May) come early summer wildflowers (May and June). Here it was necessary to make an especially arbitrary selection of what to include as spring wildflowers. Keep in mind this and the other limitations imposed and hopefully you will find most of the Bay Region's spring wildflowers, as defined, in this book.

ACTIVITIES

Many of the nature activities described on pages 45–49 of the first book in this series (Smith, 1959) fit into the study and enjoyment of wildflowers. Just sitting and looking at wildflowers with a hand-lens, for instance, can open a whole new world of aesthetic beauty. Photographing wildflowers is such a popular activity it scarcely needs mention, yet if one strives for technical and artistic perfection it can become one of the most demanding (and expensive) of hobbies. Sketching or painting wildflowers in nature is another activity with endless possibilities. So, too, is the art of flower preservation (see How-to-do-it References, p. 181). Below in some detail are just a few of the activities one can undertake when studying wildflowers.

TRIPS AFIELD

Wildflowers, like all living things, are best seen and studied in their native habitats, and springtime trips afield to see the wildflowers have been popular since the horse and buggy days. In recent years accelerated urbanization has greatly diminished the areas available to wildflowers, and a few species have gone the way of the Dodo. Nevertheless, every "good" spring still brings lavish displays in many areas. It would be difficult to exhaust in many seasons the excursions possible by car alone or by car and foot. For ideas on planning Bay Region trips afield, refer to map, p. 4, for a few hints and also consult pages 62–65 of Smith (1959). Consult pages 60–61 of Smith for good manners in the field. Or better, carry Smith's book with you as a companion to this or other books in the California Natural History Guide series.

[7]

Over 170 years ago the first of a long series of European collectors began the exploration of California's floral wealth. They took not only specimens for scientific study, but seeds — particularly seeds of annual wild-flowers. These were grown in England and later on the Continent and very soon made an enormous impact on the field of horticulture. Gardens, once strong in perennials, became dominated by annuals—the spring-time annuals of California. California's gardeners, unfortunately, have never realized the endless possibilities for experimentation in the raising of their state's native wildflowers.

To grow wildflowers it is necessary, of course, to simulate the natural habitat closely and to give special care to the plants during their early, critical period of growth (from seed-germination until the seedlings are well-established). If this is done, many of our annual wildflowers are quite easy to grow from seed. Try it; even a partial return on your efforts will seem a handsome reward. Nature provides wildflower seeds in great quantities, and if you gather your own, make certain that the fruits and their contained seeds are fully ripe. Surer, perhaps, is to purchase your seeds; see second paragraph below.

Perennial wildflowers may be grown from seed, too, but it takes several years for them to reach maturity and transplanting achieves faster results. If a garden habitat is provided which is close to the natural one, it takes only a small portion of underground stem or root to start a perennial. Emphatically, however, discrimination must be used in removing even portions of living plants from the natural scene. See again good manners for collectors, pages 60–61, Smith (1959). Never take bulbs; the lily-like plants producing them are becoming rare. Grow these plants from seed or

[8]

purchase the bulbs. Other living native perennials may also be purchased.

Commercially packaged mixtures of wildflower seeds may include many exotics, but there are a few horticulturalists who specialize in native seeds or in native bulbs or living perennials; for a source from which to obtain their addresses, see Suggestions, p. 178. See both Suggestions and References, p. 179, for sources of information on culture of wildflowers, annual or perennial.

Making an Herbarium

A miniature wildflower herbarium (collection of dried plant specimens) serves many study uses. A plant press for drying the specimens is easily assembled. Two 8 × 12-inch pieces of 1/4-inch plywood make the frames. Between these go 15 to 20 or more blotters, as many corrugates, and some folded newssheets, all items cut to fit the frames. Two 1/2-inch straps several feet long hold the press together. Cut the blotters from desk blotters or roofing felt, the corrugates from corrugated cardboard cartons, and the folded newssheets from ordinary newspaper. To use the press, place a frame on the bottom, then a corrugate, a blotter, a folded newssheet with specimen inside, a blotter, a corrugate, etc. Put the second frame on top, and strap the press tightly.

Rapid drying is essential for color-retention in specimens. Although a tightly strapped press is aerated by its corrugates, it should be dismantled daily. Do not disturb the wet plants within their folded newssheets, but remove the blotters and corrugates, dry them quickly by sun or artificial heat, and while hot return them in original sequence to the press, restrapping tightly. It takes several days to dry most plants.

If the plants are small, put several whole plants (from one collection site only) between one folded newssheet, spreading them out to avoid overlapping. If large, take a flowering branch or two and if possible some basal

[9]

parts (use a small trowel). All specimens should be in flower and/or fruit and should be representative of the living plant. On the newssheet write any notes on size, flower-color, type of habitat, and place and date of collection. Add the name of the plant when you learn what it is. Or write all data in a notebook, give each collection a number, and number the newssheet and notebook to correspond.

For easy reference the dried specimens may later be mounted on heavy paper by means of narrow strips of gummed cloth or tape (cellophane deteriorates) and filed in a looseleaf notebook. A label giving the name of the plant, collection data, and collector's name should go in the lower right-hand corner.

The above is a simplification of methods used by botanists in collecting and preparing herbarium specimens. Botanists regard their specimens as vouchers for the living plants and put them in established herbaria which serve as museum repositories where curators care for and make specimens available for study much as librarians handle the books of a library. The amateur collector who wants to learn professional collecting and mounting techniques will find that patience, a willingness to do careful work, and accuracy in assembling the data are essential. See p. 178 for a brochure on how to collect. Standard size collecting and mounting supplies can be purchased from biological supply companies or from major paper supply dealers. See p. 179 for two excellent references—Harrington (1957) and Lawrence (1955).

NAMING WILDFLOWERS

Most of this book is devoted to the most tantalizing activity of all — identifying (naming) spring wildflowers. Many folk, book in hand, will do this "in the field" where the wildflowers grow. Others will prefer to bag their wildflowers (literally) and identify them later at home. For this, go prepared with plastic bags, put an adequate sample of each plant in a separate bag, insert notes on habitat and locality, and close bag with an elastic band. Bagged plants will remain fresh in a refrigerator for about a week. Still other folk will press their plants while in the field (see preceding section) and identify them dried. Identifying dried plants is more difficult, but flowers will rejuvenate when soaked in water to which a little detergent is added to speed "wetting."

As a geologist's pick is to the rockhound and binoculars are to the bird-watcher, so a hand-lens is to the aspiring botanist—his badge. A hand-lens of × 10 or × 14 magnifying power is, indeed, almost indispensable in identifying wildflowers; it should have either a Coddington-type lens or, better, a Hastings triplet lens.

In addition to the always helpful use of illustrations, several arrangements for the identication of wildflowers are possible in a popular handbook. The simplest is to arrange the wildflowers in groups by flower-color, for which the user needs no knowledge of floral parts. Unfortunately, this arrangement ignores structural affinities and puts closely related plants into separate groups merely because they differ in flower-color. A different approach is to group plants by biotic communities — wildflowers of Grassland, Oak Woodland, etc. This, too, obscures structural affinities, but it does express environmental relationships. Our wildflowers, however, are not sufficiently limited in their environmental needs to make this a workable arrangement (see next section).

The arrangement used in this book is based primarily on plant structure, especially of flowers and fruits, and related species are brought together into the families and genera to which they belong. In addition most plants are illustrated. The method of identification is demanding, for you must see and interpret correctly floral structures, learn a few technical terms, and learn to use a key. It is also the most rewarding way to identify plants, for you will learn different floral patterns, gain a feeling of relationships, names will become more than handles, and you will be on your way to an understanding and genuine appreciation of the world of wildflowers. For instruction, turn to "How to Use the Key and Descriptive List," p. 15.

SPRING WILDFLOWERS
IN THEIR NATURAL HAUNTS

Smith (1959) describes sixteen communities of plants and animals for the San Francisco Bay Region. Each of these natural biotic communities has a distinctive set of environmental conditions (climate, water, soil, etc.) and as a result harbors a somewhat distinctive set of plants and animals.

In each community there are a few highly characteristic species of plants which have such restrictive growth requirements that they cannot grow beyond the environmental conditions found within the one community to which they are limited; these are the "indicator" species of each community. Most species, however, have less restrictive growth requirements and can grow under a range of environmental conditions common to two or three different communities. And a few species are so tolerant ("plastic") in their growth requirements that they can grow under very diverse environmental conditions such as embrace many different communities.

Spring wildflowers occur in all Bay Region communities except the Rocky Shore. Usually they are sufficiently plastic to be able to grow in two or three communities, hence they are seldom the indicator species of a community. This role is usually taken by woody plants, as in Oak Woodland where all plant indicators are trees and shrubs. In spring the grassy areas between Oak Woodland's trees and shrubs are brightened with many species of wildflowers, but none is limited to this community. Coastal Strand, on the other hand, is one community in which wildflowers *are* some of the most distinctive species, among the indicators being the two sand verbenas, the Dune Sun Cup, and the Beach Morning Glory, all lending bright color to the shifting sands and aiding in their stabilization.

A few of the most characteristic spring wildflowers of each biotic community are listed below by scientific name. Asterisks mark the indicator species. All other species occur in two or more communities.[1] The Redwood and Douglas Fir forests are treated as a unit since the wildflowers found in both are essentially the same.

COASTAL STRAND
Abronia, both species*
Convolvulus soldanella*
Oenothera cheiranthifolia*

COASTAL SALT MARSH
Amsinckia spectabilis
Potentilla egedei var. grandis
Spergularia macrotheca

FRESHWATER MARSH
Brodiaea hyacinthina*
Camassia quamash*
Lupinus polyphyllus
Mimulus guttatus
Ranunculus bloomeri
Sisyrinchium californicum*

COASTAL SCRUB
Arabis blepharophylla
Armeria maritima var.
  californica
Castilleja franciscana
Castilleja wightii
Delphinium decorum*
Erigeron glaucus

Fragaria chiloensis
Orthocarpus floribundus*

CLOSED CONE PINE
FOREST
Heuchera micrantha
Saxifraga californica

REDWOOD-DOUGLAS
FIR FORESTS
Anemone quinquefolia var.
  grayi
Asarum caudatum*
Clintonia andrewsiana
  (Redw. For.*)
Disporum, both species
Oxalis oregana*
Satureja douglasii
Scoliopus bigelovii
  (Redw. For.*)
Tiarella unifoliata
  (Redw. For.*)
Trientalis latifolia
Trillium ovatum
Vancouveria planipetala
  (Redw. For.*)
Viola sempervirens

[1] The Descriptive List (p. 40) gives all the communities in which each species usually occurs in the Bay Region.

PONDEROSA PINE FOREST

Calochortus amabilis
Fritillaria lanceolata
Pedicularis densiflora
Scutellaria tuberosa

BROADLEAF EVERGREEN FOREST

Aquilegia formosa var. truncata
Cynoglossum grande
Delphinium nudicaule
Fragaria californica
Smilacina, both species
Trillium chloropetalum

OAK WOODLAND

Calochortus albus
Clarkia concinna
Collinsia heterophylla
Delphinium patens
Dentaria californica var.
  californica
Erysimum capitatum
Gilia achilleaefolia
Nemophila heterophylla

CHAPARRAL

Allium falcifolium
Calochortus pulchellus
Calochortus umbellatus
Castilleja foliolosa*
Convolvulus occidentalis
Delphinium californicum
Zigadenus fremontii

GRASSLAND

Baeria chrysostoma
Brodiaea laxa
Calochortus venustus

Dentaria californica var.
  integrifolia
Eschscholzia californica
Gilia tricolor
Layia, all species
Limnanthes douglasii
Linanthus, most species
Lotus, most species
Microseris, both species
Monolopia major*
Nemophila menziesii
Orthocarpus, most species
Platystemon californicus
Plagiobothrys nothofulvus
Sanicula, most species
Sidalcea malvaeflora
Sisyrinchium bellum
Trifolium, most species

RIPARIAN WOODLAND

Dicentra formosa*
Mimulus guttatus
Petasites palmatus
Viola glabella

RURAL

Amsinckia intermedia
Calandrinia ciliata var.
  menziesii
Montia perfoliata
Nemophila menziesii

URBAN

Achillea millefolium, garden
  weed
Cardamine oligosperma,
  garden weed
Eschscholzia californica,
  waste places
Tellima grandiflora, garden
  escape

HOW TO USE THE KEY AND
DESCRIPTIVE LIST

Merely by looking at the pictures you can name many wildflowers in this book, but the Key will enable you to find the name of any wildflower in the Descriptive List (except inconspicuous or rare ones, given in small type). The Key (p. 20) is built of pairs of opposing statements with the same indentation and identifying letters (A, AA; etc.). One statement of a pair applies to the wildflower you are naming, and one does not. With each pair of statements you must choose the correct one and go on to the next pair. There is a short Key to Major Groups and a long Key to Species. Use the short Key first and decide to which of the four major groups your wildflower belongs. Then proceed directly to that group in the Key to Species. Technical terms are few and the drawings in Plant Parts Illustrated (p. 16) will help you to understand them. For more information on use of keys, see Harrington (1957) and Lawrence (1955).

The Key and the Descriptive List complement each other. Characters which lead you to each species in the Key are not necessarily repeated in the Descriptive List. Learn to refer to both even if you identify a plant by picture alone. Species appear in almost the same order in both, an order of relationship ending with the plants of the Sunflower Family.

The Key gives the scientific name of each species, while the Descriptive List gives both scientific and common names. When using common names, it must be kept in mind that they often vary in usage in different areas or by different people in the same area. Preferably they are vernacular or folk names and rich in romantic lore (Solomon's Seal, Miner's Lettuce). Where true folk names are lacking, the genus (first part of the scientific name) may be used for a common name (Delphinium, Penstemon), or botanists may coin

PLANT PARTS ILLUSTRATED

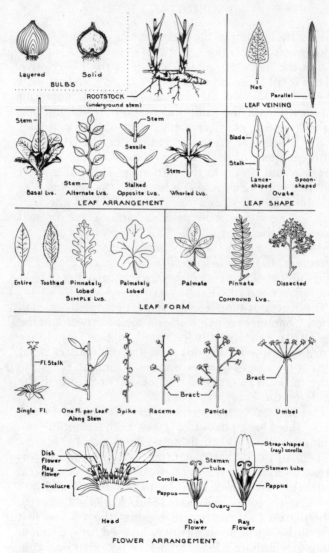

Fig. A

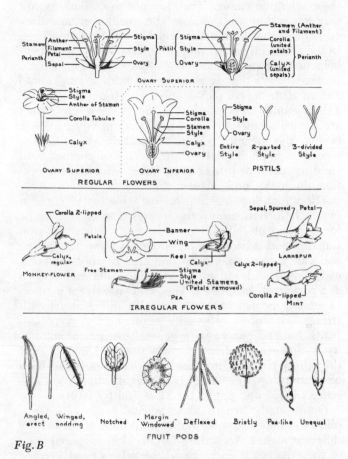

Fig. B

a common name (Contorted Sun Cup, Short-pod Trefoil).

The scientific name consists of two Latin or Latin-
ized (or Greek) words; the first (capitalized) is the
name of the genus (generic name), the second is the
name of the species (specific name). A few plants have
a third (varietal or subspecific) name. Try to learn

these scientific names. They are not so difficult as you may think, they are the same the world over, and they do help in developing the feel for plant relationships. In the Descriptive List they are marked with accents to help in their pronunciation (a grave accent à over a stressed vowel that is pronounced with a long sound and an acute accent á over one that is pronounced with a short sound). It is interesting, too, to know why plants are named as they are, and the Descriptive List gives, briefly, the meaning of most scientific names. These give clues to plant relationships, which, if pursued, will yield a wealth of information about scientific exploration, discovery, and history.

The scientific name represents a biological concept in which the basic unit is the *species*. The species stands for a group of individuals very much alike and presumably with a common parentage. If a species is large and varies somewhat from one area to another, botanists may "divide" it into subspecific units each known as a *variety* or *subspecies*. The *genus* stands for a group of related species, each recognizably different yet with strong similarities especially evident in flowers and fruits. Related genera with general features of similarity in flowers and fruits form a *family*. Don't neglect the family concept; it is useful in learning broad lines of relationship. For more about classification, see Lawrence (1955) and pages 18–21 of Smith (1959).

Occasionally two or more scientific names get applied to one species so that it may become known by different names. According to botanical rules only one of these names is correct and the others must become synonyms. If any of our wildflowers has been well-known by a name now recognized as a synonym, the synonym appears in the Descriptive List in brackets following the accepted scientific name.

In the Descriptive List a species may be the sole member of its genus or of its family, or there may be two or more species in a genus or two or more genera in a family; if the latter, the characters common to all species in the group are briefly stated under the genus or family. Look for these generic and family descriptions; they will help in identification of the species.

A statement of habitat, biotic communities occupied, and usual months of flowering is given for every species in the Descriptive List except for some of the inconspicuous or rare ones (those in small type). To help in their location in the Descriptive List, species are numbered in both Key and Descriptive List if there are more than three in a genus. The magnification on each figure refers to the habit sketch, not to the enlarged flower or fruit.

Abbreviations

ca.: approximately
Co., Cos.: County, Counties
e.: east, eastern
fl., fls.: flower, -s
fig.: figure
fr., frs.: fruit, -s
ft.: foot, feet
in.: inch, inches
lf., lvs.: leaf, leaves
n.: north, northern
occas.: occasional, -ly
p., pp.: page, -s

s.: south, southern
sev.: several
S.F.: San Francisco
spp.: species (more than 1)
subsp.: subspecies
var.: variety (of a species)
w.: west, western
+: plus, over, more than
−: minus, under, less than
±: more-or-less
−: to (8–12; Apr.–May)

Abbreviations Used for Biotic Communities
(listed in order in which cited)

Cst. Str.: Coastal Strand
Cst. Salt Marsh: Coastal Salt Marsh
Fresh. Marsh: Freshwater Marsh
Cst. Scr.: Coastal Scrub
Cl. C. Pine For.: Closed Cone Pine Forest
Redw.-Doug. Fir For.: Redwood-Douglas Fir Forests

Pon. Pine For.: Ponderosa Pine Forest
Bd. Ev. For.: Broadleaf Evergreen Forest
Oak Wood.: Oak Woodland
Chap.: Chaparral
Grass.: Grassland
Riparian Wood.: Riparian Woodland
Rur.: Rural
Urb.: Urban

KEY TO SPRING WILDFLOWERS OF SAN FRANCISCO BAY REGION

A Fl. parts in 3's or multiples of 3; lvs. simple and usually with 3 or more lengthwise parallel veins (hold leaf to light to see obscure veins); underground bulbs often present.
MONOCOTYLEDONS, **Group 1**

AA Fl. parts rarely in 3's, mostly in 4's or 5's, or sometimes numerous; lvs. simple or compound, with netted or inconspicuous veins; bulbs not present.   DICOTYLEDONS
    B Fls. with perianth segments all alike and either sepal-like or petal-like in color and texture. **Group 2**, p. 23
    BB Fls. with perianth segments in 2 usually unlike series— sepals or calyx (outer series) and petals or corolla (inner series); calyx small (or occas. lacking).
        C Petals free or almost free from each other, usually falling separately. . . . .**Group 3**, p. 24
        CC Petals joined to form a lobed corolla which falls as a unit. . . . .**Group 4**, p. 33

Key to Species

MONOCOTYLEDONS, Group 1

A Ovary superior (sepals and petals, i.e., outer 3 and inner 3 perianth segments, attached around ovary at its base; ovary visible in center of fl.).   (p. 22 for AA)
    B Lvs. on stem or at base of plant; fls. sev.–many in a raceme or panicle, or occas. single or in sev. loose bractless clusters of 2–5 fls.   (**Liliaceae**)
            (p. 22 for BB)
        C Sepals and petals very much alike.
           D Fls. white to greenish or creamy white.
              E Fls. drooping or nodding.
                F Stem branched; fls. 1–5 in clusters below branch-tips.
                  (*Disporum*, p. 48)
                  G Fls. 1/2–5/8 in. long; style entire; common, woods. . . .*D. hookeri*
                  GG Fls. 3/4–1 in. long; style 3-lobed; coastal forests. . . . . . .*D. smithii*
                FF Stem unbranched; fls. 1–5 in a raceme at stem-tip. *Fritillaria liliacea*, p. 46

EE Fls. erect, not drooping or nodding.
 F Lvs. all about same size, ovate, alter-
  nate on stem. (*Smilacina*, p. 47)
  G Fls. in a panicle......*S. racemosa*
  GG Fls. in a raceme........*S. stellata*
 FF Basal lvs. long, narrow, the stem lvs.
  small, few. ....
     Zigadenus fremontii, p. 41
DD Fls. blue, red, or brownish purple.
 E Fls. deep blue; wet meadows, Marin and
  Sonoma Cos...*Camassia quamash*, p. 42
 EE Fls. red or brownish purple.
  F Fls. deep red; Redw. For. ....
    Clintonia andrewsiana, p. 49
  FF Fls. brownish purple; wooded areas.
    Fritillaria lanceolata, p. 46
CC Sepals and petals unlike in color and/or in size and
shape.
 D Lvs. 2, basal; sepals greenish with brownish-
  purple veins, larger than the dark-purplish
  petals; stamens 3. *Scoliopus bigelovii*, p. 50
 DD Lvs. usually more than 2; sepals green, greenish, or colored like petals, but smaller than
  petals; stamens 6.
  E Lvs. broad, 3 in a circle at stem-tip; fl. 1;
   petals plain, hairless. (*Trillium*, p. 51)
  F Fl. sessile (stalkless); petals deep red
   (occas. white)... *T. chloropetalum*
  FF Fl. on a slender stalk; petals white,
   aging pink or rose.......*T. ovatum*
  EE Lvs. long, narrow, usually 1 at base and
   smaller ones alternate on stems; fls. 1-
   sev.; petals often elaborately marked,
   often hairy within. (*Calochortus*, p. 42)
  F Fls. erect, open, bell-shaped.
   G Pods erect, 3-angled; basal leaf or
    lvs. shorter than stem, soon
    withering. (Mariposa lilies)
    H Petals white to purplish (oc-
     cas. yellow), red-blotched;
     gland (nectary at petal
     base) square. ....
       1. *C. venustus*

HH Petals yellow, occas. with a
    red-brown blotch; gland
    crescent-shaped. . . . .
                        2. *C. luteus*
GG Pods nodding, 3-winged; basal leaf
    1, longer than stem, remaining
    green; petals white to lilac.
                        (star tulips)
    H Petals with a few hairs inside
        near base. 3. *C. umbellatus*
    HH Petals hairy on inner surface
        to tip. . . . . . . .4. *C. tolmiei*
FF Fls. nodding, globe-shaped, the petals
    incurved; pods nodding, 3-winged;
    basal leaf 1, equalling stem, remain-
    ing green. . . . .(globe lilies)
    G Fls. white or pearly, often red-
        purplish near base. 5. *C. albus*
    GG Fls. yellow.
        H Petals hairy within to near
            tip; Mt. Diablo. . . . .
                        6. *C. pulchellus*
        HH Petals hairy within only near
            base; Marin, Napa, Sonoma
            Cos. . . . . . . .7. *C. amabilis*
BB Lvs. all basal; fls. all at tip of stem in 1 loose or tight
    cluster (umbel) beneath which are 1–sev. papery bracts.
                        (**Amaryllidaceae**)
    C Onion odor; fls. pink to rose; sepals and petals free
        from each other or nearly so.   (*Allium*, p. 52)
        D Stem flat, 4–6 in. tall. . . . .*A. falcifolium*
        DD Stem round, 8–12 in. tall. . . . .*A. serratum*
    CC Without onion odor; fls. white or blue; sepals and
        petals joined at base.   (*Brodiaea*, p. 54)
        D Fls. white; wet low places. 1. *B. hyacinthina*
        DD Fls. blue or violet-blue; habitats various.
            E Fls. in a tight umbel.
                F Stamens 6; Feb.–Apr.. .2. *B. pulchella*
                FF Stamens 3; Apr.–June. 3. *B. congesta*
            EE Fls. in a loose umbel. . . . . .4. *B. laxa*
AA Ovary inferior (sepals and petals, i.e., outer 3 and inner 3
    perianth segments, attached at top of ovary; ovary visible
    below sepals and petals).
    B Fls. regular (petals and/or sepals all same shape).
                        (**Iridaceae**)

[22]

C Stem round; sepals same color as petals, but of different size and shape; styles 3, petal-like.

(*Iris*, p. 57)

D Tube below sepals and petals over 1/2 in. long; wooded areas or grasslands.

E Tube 3/4–1 in. long. . . . . . .*I. douglasiana*
EE Tube 1½–4 in. long. . . . . .*I. macrosiphon*

DD Tube below sepals and petals less than 1/2 in. long; coastal grasslands. . . . . . .*I. longipetala*

CC Stem flat; sepals and petals alike; style 3-lobed, not petal-like. (*Sisyrinchium*, p. 56)

D Fls. blue; grasslands, common. . . . . .*S. bellum*
DD Fls. yellow; coastal marshes. . . .*S. californicum*

BB Fls. irregular (petals not all same shape, in this case 1 enlarged and sac-like or tubular).

Orchidaceae, p. 58

DICOTYLEDONS

Group 2

(PERIANTH SEGMENTS ALL ALIKE, SEPAL-LIKE OR PETAL-LIKE)

A Perianth segments free from each other, often falling early; stamens many (more than 12). (**Ranunculaceae**)

B Lvs. 3 (each with 3 leaflets) near stem-tip; fl. 1, white or bluish . . . .*Anemone quinquefolia*, p. 72

BB Lvs. more than 3 (each with many leaflets), alternate along stem; fls. many in a raceme or panicle.

C Fls. green, in a panicle. *Thalictrum polycarpum*, p. 72

CC Fls. creamy white, in a raceme. *Actaea arguta*, p. 67

AA Perianth segments joined below into a tube, their lobes (tips) free, not falling early; stamen 5–12.

B Lvs. heart-shaped; fls. purple-brown; Redw.-Doug. Fir For. . . . .*Asarum caudatum*, p. 59

BB Lvs. not heart-shaped; fls. white, pink, or yellow, with an involucre (circle of separate or united bracts) at base of fl.-cluster.

C Fls. many in tight clusters (heads), with an involucre of sev. *separate* bracts at base of cluster; stems prostrate; seashore. (*Abronia*, p. 61)

D Fls. yellow . . . .*A. latifolia*
DD Fls. rose-pink. . . . .*A. umbellata*

CC Fls. 1–sev. within an involucre of *united* bracts; stems erect; mostly inland. (**Polygonaceae**)

[23]

D Involucre bowl-shaped, with 6 hooked spines;
fls. hidden. *Chorizanthe membranacea,* p. 60
DD Involucre tubular, with 6 short lobes; fls. protruding . . . . *Eriogonum* spp., p. 61

The following may seem to belong to Group 2, as perianth seg-
ments may seem to be in 1 series. Look for plants as indicated.
A Fls. minute; sepals 4; petals sometimes 0; stamens 6.
(*Athysanus,* Group 3, p. 27)
AA Not as above.
B Sepals petal-like, they and petals 6 each, white, and
abruptly turned back. (*Vancouveria,* Group 3,below)
BB Sepals, if present, not as above.
C Fls. in an umbel; sepals occas. absent; petals 5,
free to base. (**Umbelliferae,** Group 3, p. 28)
CC Fls. in a dense head encircled at base by green
bracts, the whole simulating a single fl.; sepals
absent or highly modified; petals joined into a
tubular or strap-like corolla.
(**Compositae,** Group 4, p. 38)

Group 3
(Petals free from each other)

1 Fl. regular — all petals alike in shape, all sepals alike in shape
(p. 30 for 2)

*(a) Sepals the same color and texture as petals and often also
similar to petals in size and shape*

[p. 25 for *(aa)*]

A Sepals and petals 4 each, the sepals sometimes the same
color as petals. (**Cruciferae,** see D, p. 26)
AA Sepals and petals not 4 each.
B Stamens 6, pressed to pistil; sepals and petals white,
turned backward. . . . . *Vancouveria planipetala,* p. 74
BB Stamens many; sepals and petals various, not as above.
C Lvs. entire, in a tuft on ground; fls. white to pink;
petals 13–15. . . . . *Lewisia rediviva,* p. 64
CC Lvs. lobed to compound, mostly on above-ground
stems; petals 5–10. (**Ranunculaceae**)
D Fls. in a raceme at stem-tip, white; sepals and
petals falling early. . . . . . . *Actaea arguta,* p. 67
DD Fls. scattered near branch-tips.
E Fls. red with yellow; petals each with a
long spur (slender nectar-secreting sac).
Aquilegia formosa, p. 67

[24]

EE Fls. yellow; petals not spurred.

(*Ranunculus,* see EE, p. 26)

(aa) Sepals not same color and texture as petals, but green or greenish and of different size and shape

A Sepals 2 (or seemingly 1) or 3.
    B Petals orange, yellow, or red; stamens 5–many.
        C Sepals 2; petals 5 (or 3–7), red-purple; stamens 5–14 ....*Calandrinia ciliata,* p. 62
        CC Sepals 2 or 3, falling early (look at buds); petals 4 or 6; stamens many. (**Papaveraceae**)
            D Sepals 3, free from each other; petals 6, cream or yellow.....*Platystemon californicus,* p. 75
            DD Sepals 2, free from each other or fused and seemingly 1; petals 4.
                E Sepals free; petals orange-red ....
                    Stylomecon heterophylla, p. 76
                EE Sepals fused into a pointed cap; petals orange to orange-yellow. ....
                    Eschscholzia californica, p. 77
    BB Sepals 2; petals white to pink; stamens 5. (*Montia,* p. 63)
        C Stem-lvs. more than 2, alternate on stem; Redw.-Doug. Fir For. ....*M. parvifolia*
        CC Stem-lvs. 2, opposite at top of stem, partly or entirely fused; habitats various.
            D Stem-lvs. fused to form a large concave disk; petals white. ....*M. perfoliata*
            DD Stem-lvs. fused only near base or on 1 side only; petals pink ....*M. spathulata*

AA Sepals (or calyx-lobes) 4 or 5.
    B Stamens many (more than 10); sepals 5.
        C Filaments of stamens united into a tube around pistil ....*Sidalcea malvaeflora,* p. 111
        CC Filaments of stamens free from each other to base.
            D Lvs. and stems rough-hairy; fls. 1½–3 in. wide.
                Mentzelia lindleyi, p. 115
            DD Lacking rough hairs; fls. 1/2–1 in. wide.
                E Sepals alternating with 5 small bractlets (tiny leaf-like structures). (**Rosaceae**)
                  F Lvs. each with 3 leaflets; petals white.
                    (*Fragaria,* p. 94)
                    G Lvs. thick; coastal. ..*F. chiloensis*
                    GG Lvs. thin; woods ...*F. californica*

FF Lvs. with more than 3 leaflets; petals yellow. (*Potentilla*, p. 95)

G Leaflets green on both sides; habitats various .....*P. glandulosa*

GG Leaflets silvery-silky beneath; salt marshes ....*P. egedei*

EE Sepals without alternating bractlets; petals yellow. (*Ranunculus*, p. 73)

F Fls. *ca.* 1/2–1 in. across.

G. Plants ± hairy; common, grassy or wooded areas. *R. californicus*

GG Plants hairless; uncommon, wet meadows, marshes .*R. bloomeri*

FF Fls. less than 1/4 in. wide; woods. ...
R. hebecarpus

BB Stamens 4–10; sepals (or calyx-lobes) 4 or 5.

C Sepals and petals 4 each. (p. 28 for CC)

D Stamens 6 (4 long, 2 short); ovary superior (attached above bases of sepals and petals and visible within fl.) (**Cruciferae**[2])
(p. 27 for DD)

E Lvs. arrow-shaped, very numerous, almost hiding stem ....*Arabis glabra*, p. 83

EE Lvs. not as above.

F Petals cream to yellow or orange.

G Lvs. deeply lobed; petals yellow. .
Barbarea orthoceras, p. 81

GG Lvs. entire or dentate.
(*Erysimum*, p. 84)

H Petals orange; dry, mostly inland slopes ..*E. capitatum*

HH Petals cream to yellow; seaward slopes ....
E. franciscanum

FF Petals white to pink, rose, or purple.

G Plant fleshy; coastal sand-dunes.
Cakile edentula, p. 81

GG Plant not fleshy; not on sanddunes. (*move left for* H)

H Petals deep rose-purple to pink; rocks near coast ......
Arabis blepharophylla, p. 84

[2] Some with minute fls. may lack petals or a pair of stamens.

HH Petals white to light pinkish lavender.
  I Pods round, to 1/4 in. long; fls. tiny.
    J Pods without hairs, notched at tip . . . .
                     Lepidium nitidum, p. 86
    JJ Pods usually dull-hairy; not obviously notched at
       tip.
       K Pod-margins with radiating nerves, often also
         "windowed." . . . .
                  Thysanocarpus curvipes, p. 87
      KK Pod-margins plain . *Athysanus pusillus*, p. 86
  II Pods long (1–2 in.), narrow.
    J Pods bent down; fls. 1/8–1/4 in. long. . . . .
            Thelypodium lasiophyllum, p. 79
    JJ Pods erect or merely spreading.
      K Fls. minute, *ca*. 1/8 in. long; lvs. with *ca*. 7–9
       round leaflets. . . . .
              Cardamine oligosperma, p. 82
      KK Fls. 3/8–1/2 in. long; lvs. irregularly toothed or
       with 3–5 leaflets.
        L Lvs. without hairs; stem unbranched . . . .
             Dentaria californica, p. 82
        LL Lvs. rough-hairy; stem usually branched.
          Streptanthus glandulosus, p. 80
DD Stamens 4 or 8 (sometimes 4 long, 4 short);
   ovary inferior (at base of fl. below attachment of sepals and petals), sometimes with
   a short or very long tube between ovary and
   sepals and petals.   (**Onagraceae**)
  E Petals deeply notched at tip, pink to rose;
    stamens 8. . . . *Epilobium franciscanum*,
                       p. 116
  EE Petals 3-lobed or rounded.
    F Petals pink or lavender to rose or pur-
      ple.   (*Clarkia*, p. 116)
      G Petals 3-lobed; stamens 4. . . . . . .
                     C. concinna
      GG Petals entire; stamens 8.
        H Petals each with a long, nar-
         row, basal claw. . . . .
                 C. unguiculata
        HH Petals narrowed gradually to
         base . . . .*C. gracilis*,
        C. amoena, and *C. purpurea*
    FF Petals yellow, reddish with age; sta-
    mens 8.   (*Oenothera*, p. 117)
      G Lvs. (at least some) basal and in

a rosette (circle) on ground.

H Both basal lvs. and leafy prostrate fl.-stems present;
beach-sands. 2. . . . .
O. cheiranthifolia

HH No leafy stems; all lvs. basal;
grassland . . . . . . 1. *O. ovata*

GG All lvs. on stem, none basal.

H Pods 4-sided. 3. *O. micrantha*

HH Pods cylindric. 4. *O. contorta*

CC Sepals (or calyx-lobes) and petals 5 each.

D Lvs. parsley-like, their stalks with dilated bases;
fls. yellow, white, or greenish (purple in 1),
tiny and numerous in umbels or heads (loose
or tight clusters); ovary inferior (below
corolla). (**Umbelliferae**) (p. 29 for DD)

E Frs. roundish, not much longer than wide.

F Frs. bristly or scaly; lvs. lobed or divided but the divisions not numerous. (*Sanicula*, p. 120)

G Plant yellowish green, prostrate or
nearly so. . . . . .1. *S. arctopoides*

GG Plant bright green, erect.

H Basal lvs. palmately lobed.

I Plant 1–3 ft. tall, robust.
2. *S. crassicaulis*

II Plant 1/2–1 ft. tall, not
robust. . . . 3. *S. laciniata*

HH Basal lvs. pinnately lobed or
compound.

I Fls. purple. . . . .
4. *S. bipinnatifida*

II Fls. yellow.

J Frs. with hooked bris-
tles. 5. *S. bipinnata*

JJ Frs. with swollen
scales . 6. *S. tuberosa*

FF Frs. not bristly or scaly (but sometimes
hairy).

G Stem 4–5 ft. tall; lvs. with 3 large
leaflets . . . *Heracleum lanatum*,
p. 124

GG Stem 1/2–2 ft. tall; lvs. much
divided. (*Lomatium*, p. 123)

[28]

H Petals yellow. *L. utriculatum*
HH Petals white or greenish. . . . .
L. dasycarpum
EE Frs. linear, sev. times longer than wide. . . .
Osmorhiza chilensis, p. 122
DD Lvs. not parsley-like (although dissected in
Limnanthes); fls. white, pink or red, variously
arranged, but if in umbels *(Dodecatheon)* or
in heads *(Armeria),* then fls. pink; ovary su-
perior (attached above base of calyx and
corolla).
E Stamens and petals 5 each; lvs. basal.
F Lvs. linear, leathery; fls. pink, in heads.
Armeria maritima, p. 127
FF Lvs. broad, thin; fls. white, in a panicle.
(**Saxifragaceae**)
G Each fl. branch of the panicle with
a small lf. at its base. . . . .
Boykinia elata, p. 90
GG Each fl.-branch with a narrow
bract at its base. . . . .
Heuchera micrantha, p. 92
(*move left for* EE)
EE Stamens 10, petals 5; lvs. basal or on stem.
F Lvs. opposite (or seeming to be whorled), 2 (to sev.)
at each node (joint) of stem.   (**Caryophyllaceae**)
G Fls. red. . . . .*Silene californica*, p. 66
GG Fls. white or light pink.
H Plant somewhat glandular-hairy; coastal.
I Lvs. lance-shaped; fls. white. . . . .
Cerastium arvense, p. 65
II Lvs. linear; fls. pink. . . . .
Spergularia macrotheca, p. 66
HH Plant not glandular or hairy; fls. white; dry
rocky areas. . . . . . .*Arenaria douglasii*, p. 65
FF Lvs. basal or alternate on stem.
G Lvs. with 3 heart-shaped leaflets; fls. pink. . . . . . .
Oxalis oregana, p. 110
GG Lvs. not as above.
H Lvs. dissected, alternate; fls. white and yellow.
Limnanthes douglasii, p. 111
HH Lvs. simple, mostly basal.
I Plant very fleshy; fls. yellow. . . . .
Sedum spathulifolium, p. 87
II Plant not fleshy; fls. white to red.
(**Saxifragaceae**)

J Petals lobed or fringed.
K Petals fringed along sides, whitish
fading red; styles 2. . . . .
Tellima grandiflora, p. 91
KK Petals lobed on upper half, white or
faint pink; styles 3. . . . .
Lithophragma spp., p. 91
JJ Petals not lobed or fringed, white.
K Petals inconspicuous; halves of ripe
fr. very unequal. . . . .
Tiarella unifoliata, p. 90
KK Petals obvious; halves of ripe fr.
equal. *Saxifraga californica*, p. 89

**2 Fl. irregular – some petals or sepals of different shape
than others on same fl.**

A Lvs. entire; fls. single on leafless stalks.   (*Viola*, p. 112)
B Fls. yellow, sometimes dark-veined.
C Lvs. heart-shaped; moist shady forests.
D Stem creeping; forest floor. 1. *V. sempervirens*
DD Stem erect; stream banks. . . . . . .2. *V. glabella*
CC Lvs. ovate; open grassy hills. . . . .3. *V. pedunculata*
BB Fls. white, blue, violet, or red-purple.
C Fls. white and purple with yellow beard; Redw.-
Doug. Fir For. . . . . .4. *V. ocellata*
CC Fls. pale to deep violet, fading red-purple; open
coastal hills. . . . . .5. *V. adunca*

AA Lvs. deeply lobed or compound; fls. variously arranged.
B Lvs. finely dissected; fls. heart-shaped; sepals 2, small,
scale-like; stamens 6. . . . .*Dicentra formosa*, p. 78
BB Lvs. not finely dissected; fls. not heart-shaped; sepals 5
or united into a 5-lobed or 2-lipped calyx.
C Sepals 5, same color as petals or ± greenish, 1 with
long spur at base; petals 4, small, in 2 unequal
pairs; stamens many.   (*Delphinium*, p. 68)
D Plant 1/2–2½ ft. tall; fls. 1–30 per stalk.
E Fls. red. . . . . .1. *D. nudicaule*
EE Fls. blue to purple.
F Roots fleshy, easy to break from stem.
G Stem 1½–2 ft. tall, not hairy; fls.
6–20; inland. . . . . .2. *D. patens*
GG Stem 6–8 in. tall, white-hairy; fls.
1–6; coastal. . . .3. *D. decorum*
FF Roots woody, not easy to break from
stem.

[30]

G Fls. purple-blue, 3/4–1 in. wide; widespread. ...4. *D. hesperium*

GG Fls. royal purple, 1–1½ in. wide; inland. ......5. *D. variegatum*

DD Plant to 3+ ft. tall; fls. whitish, up to 50 per stalk. ....6. *D. californicum*

CC Calyx 5-lobed or 2-lipped, green, not spurred; petals 5, shaped like a Sweet-Pea, the upper petal *(banner)* largest and usually erect, the 2 side petals *(wings)* outside the 2 fused lower petals *(keel)*; stamens 10 (usually 9 with filaments united, the 10th free). **(Leguminosae)**

D Lvs. with only 3 leaflets.

E Leaflets and calyx dotted with glandular spots; fls. greenish white tipped with purple. ......*Psoralea physodes,* p. 107

EE Leaflets and calyx not glandular-dotted.

F Fls. many in a raceme, bright yellow. *Thermopsis macrophylla,* p. 97

FF Fls. single, in small umbels or in heads.

G Leaflets entire; fls. single or in umbels. *(Lotus,* see F, below)

GG Leaflets toothed; fls. in heads. (*Trifolium,* p. 103)

(*move left for* H)

H Head with an involucre of fused bracts below fls.; calyx not hairy.

I Fls. greenish white or cream, very inflated with age. ......1. *T. fucatum*

II Fls. pink to purplish, not inflated.

J Plant annual.

K Calyx-lobes abruptly pointed at tip, often bluntly toothed on each side. 2. *T. tridentatum*

KK Calyx-lobes gradually narrowed, toothless. ..3. *T. variegatum*

JJ Plant perennial; calyx-lobes needle-like, occas. with needle-like teeth. 4. *T. wormskjoldii*

HH Head without an involucre; calyx hairy; fls. purplish. ......5. *T. albopurpureum*

DD Lvs. with 4–many leaflets (occas. 3 in *Lotus*).

E Lvs. pinnately compound.

F Fls. single or in small umbels; leaflets 4–9 occas. 3. (*Lotus,* p. 105)

G Fls. bicolored, the banner yellow,
the wings and keel white to pink
or purple. 1. *L. formosissimus*
GG Fls. not bicolored, white, pink, or
yellow, fading red.
H Fls. yellow fading red; stems
± prostrate or spreading.
I Plant densely silky-hairy;
calyx-teeth longer than
tube. 3. *L. humistratus*
II Plant scantily hairy; calyx-
teeth *ca.* as long as tube.
4. *L. subpinnatus*
HH Fls. cream-white to pink, fad-
ing red.
I Plant 3–12 in. tall, not
hairy. 2. *L. micranthus*
II Plant 1/2–2 ft. tall, ±
silky-hairy. . . . .
5. *L. purshianus*
FF Fls. 1–2 or in racemes; leaflets 8–15.
G Leaflets with branched tendrils.
H Style-tip with a ring of hairs.
Vicia americana, p. 109
HH Style-tip with hairs on inner
side only. . . . .
Lathyrus vestitus, p. 109
GG Leaflets without tendrils. . . . .
Astragalus gambelianus, p. 108
EE Lvs. palmately compound; leaflets 5–9. . .
(*Lupinus*, p. 98)
(*move left for* F)
F Annual; plant 1/2–2 ft. tall; leaflets 1/2–1½ in. long.
G Seeds 2 per pod; fls. in definite whorls (circles).
H Fls. blue or violet to red-purple, erect in age. . .
1. *L. subvexus*
HH Fls. white to yellow (or tinged blue or rose), in
age turned to 1 side of stem. 2 *L. densiflorus*
GG Seeds 3–12 per pod; fls. in whorls (circles) or irregu-
larly spaced. predominantly blue to purplish.
H Stem stout, succulent, usually hollow; fls. 1/2 in.
or more long. . . . . .3. *L. succulentus*
HH Stem slender, not hollow; fls. mostly smaller.
I Fls. ± 1/2 in. long, in 3–7 whorls. 4. *L. nanus*
II Fls. ± 1/4 in. long, in 1–3 whorls. . . . .
5. *L. bicolor*

[32]

FF Perennial; plant 1½–3 ft. tall; leaflets to 8 in. long.
 G Leaflets to 4. in. long; woods. . . . . .7. *L. latifolius*
 GG Leaflets to 8 in. long; marshes. . . . .6. *L. polyphyllus*

Group 4

<small>(PETALS JOINED TO FORM A LOBED COROLLA
WHICH FALLS AS A UNIT)</small>

1 **Ovary superior (calyx and corolla attached around
ovary at its base; ovary visible in center of fl.)**
           (p. 38 for **2**)

 (a) Corolla regular (all lobes the same shape)
           [p. 36 for *(aa)*]

A Fls. in dense heads, pink, each head surrounded at base by
 a circle of dry, papery, brownish bracts; lvs. basal, leathery;
 sand-dunes, maritime bluffs. . . . *Armeria maritima*, p. 127
AA Fls. various, but if in dense heads then not as above.
 B Stamens many; filaments united into an obvious tube
  around pistil. . . . .*Sidalcea malvaeflora*, p. 111
 BB Stamens 4–10; filaments free from each other (lightly
  joined in *Dodecatheon, Solanum*).
  C Lvs. with 3 heart-shaped leaflets; stamens 10. . . . . .
           Oxalis oregana, p. 110
  CC Lvs. not as above; stamens 4 or 5 (5–7 in *Trien-
   talis*).
   D Plant twining or trailing (except in FF); corolla
    1½–2 in. long. (*Convolvulus*, p. 128)
    E Coastal sand-dunes. . . . .*C. soldanella*
    EE Grassland, brush, woods.
     F Brush or woods; climbing over shrubs.
           C. occidentalis
     FF Grassland; stems short. . .*C. subacaulis*
   DD Plant not twining or trailing; corolla smaller.
    E Fls. in small erect spikes; corolla 4-lobed,
     thin, dry, transparent; styles 5. . . . .
          Plantago erecta, p. 157
    EE Fls. variously arranged; corolla 4–5-lobed,
     not dry and transparent; style 1, entire or
     2–3 branched.
     F Stamens opposite the corolla lobes.
           (**Primulaceae**)
      G Lvs. in a tuft on ground; corolla
       cyclamen-like, reflexed.
        (*Dodecatheon*, p. 125)
       H Stamen-tube purple; wooded
        slopes. . . . .*D. hendersonii*

HH Stamen-tube purple with 5 yellow spots; grassland. . . .
D. clevelandii

GG Lvs. 3–6 in a circle at stem-tip; corolla flat, saucer-shaped. . . . .
Trientalis latifolia, p. 127

FF Stamens alternating with corolla lobes.

G Stamens conspicuous, with very short filaments and large yellow anthers in a close circle around pistil. . . . *Solanum xantii,* p. 148

GG Stamens not as above.

(move left for H *)*

H Ovary of pistil deeply 4-lobed, maturing into 1–4 separate, 1-seeded nutlets (hard frs.); style entire; lvs. simple. (**Boraginaceae**)

I Fls. blue, in very loosely coiled clusters; perennial. . . .
Cynoglossum grande, p. 140

II Fls. white or yellow to orange, in tightly coiled, 1-sided spikes; annuals.

J Fls. yellow-orange to orange. (*Amsinckia,* p. 141)

K Fls. *ca.* 1/4 in. wide; common. . . *A. intermedia*

KK Fls. 3/8–1/2 in. wide; coastal. . . *A. spectabilis*

JJ Fls. white.

K Lvs. scattered on stems; calyx not shedding its top half like a lid.

L Dry slopes. . . . . . *Cryptantha* spp., p. 142

LL Low wet fields, e. part of Bay Region. . . .
Plagiobothrys stipitatus, p. 143

KK Lvs. mostly in a flat circle on ground; calyx in fr. shedding its top-half like a lid. . . . .
Plagiobothrys nothofulvus, p. 144

HH Ovary not deeply lobed, maturing into a sev.–many-seeded capsule (dry fr.-pod); style entire or more usually 2- or 3-cleft; lvs. simple or compound.

I Calyx divided almost to base into 5 lobes (sepals); style entire or 2-cleft (to deeply 2-divided); capsule with 1–2 cavities. (**Hydrophyllaceae**)

J Fls. in tightly coiled, 1-sided spikes; style 2-cleft; lvs. alternate. (*Phacelia,* p. 137)

K Perennial; lvs. once-divided or only deeply lobed. . . . .*P. californica*

KK Annual.

L Lvs. much-divided, fern-like. . .*P. distans*

LL Lvs. entire, oblong to ovate, occas. with 2 or more small lobes. . . . .*P. divaricata*

[34]

JJ Fls. single or loosely arranged; lvs. mostly opposite.
  K Annual; calyx-lobes alternating with tiny bractlets; style 2-cleft.
    L Stem weak, 2–sev. ft. long, with hooked prickles; fls. purple, to 1 in. wide. . . . . .
    Pholistoma auritum, p. 135
    LL Stem weak but only 1/2–1½ ft. long, with recurved hairs. (*Nemophila*, p. 136)
      M Fls. white to blue, 1/2–1½ in. wide; grasslands or woods. *N. menziesii*
      MM Fls. white, 1/4–3/8 in. wide; shade in woods. . . . .*N. heterophylla*
  KK Perennial; roots white, tuberous; calyx without bractlets; style entire; fls. white; deep shade, coastal forest. *Romanzoffia suksdorfii*, p. 139
II Calyx tubular or cup-shaped, 5-lobed; style 3-cleft; capsule with 3 cavities. (**Polemoniaceae**)
  J Lvs. all alternate.
    K Fls. in dense leafy-bracted clusters; pink to rose. . . . .*Collomia heterophylla*, p. 129
    KK Fls. scattered to densely clustered but not leafy-bracted, blue to violet.
      L Lvs. simple or with 3–7 oblong or lanceolate lobes; fls. to 1/4 in. wide. . . . .
      Allophyllum spp., p. 130
      LL Lvs. compound with usually sev.–many narrow segments; fls. mostly 1/4 in. or more wide. (*Gilia*, p. 131)
        M Corolla-tube yellow with purple spots, the lobes pale blue. . . . .
        G. tricolor
        MM Corolla uniformly blue or violet.
          N Fls. usually up to 8–25 in loose clusters. . . . .*G. achilleaefolia*
          NN Fls. 50–100 in dense clusters. . .
          G. capitata
  JJ Lvs. opposite, or only the upper ones alternate.
    K Lvs. entire. . . . .*Phlox gracilis*, p. 130
    KK Lvs. fan-like (palmate) with 3–11 narrow divisions. (*Linanthus*, p. 133)
      L Fls. not in dense heads, scattered.
        M Fls. white, 3/4–1½ in. long, open in evening . . . . . . .1. *L. dichotomus*
        MM Fls. whitish to pink, blue, or lilac; 3/8–1 in. long, open in day. . . . .
        2. *L. ambiguus* or 3. *L. liniflorus*

[35]

LL Fls. in dense heads.
  M Fls. ±3/8–1/2 in. wide, white, pink,
    rose, or yellow. .4. *L. androsaceus*
  MM Fls. ±1/4 in. wide, white to pink. . .
    5. *L. ciliatus* or 6. *L. bicolor*

(aa) Corolla irregular, not all lobes the same shape

A Fls. pea-shaped, only the 2 lower petals (*keel*) united, the other 3 free; stamens 10. (**Leguminosae**) (see CC, p. 31)
AA Fls. not pea-shaped, the corolla 4–5 lobed; stamens 2–6.
 B Sepals 2; stamens 6 . . . .*Dicentra formosa*, p. 78
 BB Sepals united into a 4–5-lobed or 2-lipped calyx; stamens 2 or 4.
  C Stem square; lvs. opposite, with a mint odor (except *Scutellaria*); ovary 4-lobed, maturing into 4 1-seeded nutlets (hard frs.).   (**Labiatae**)
   D Annual or perennial with ± erect stems; fls. 1 per lf. or in often dense clusters.
    E Calyx 2-lipped, the lips entire or toothed; fls. blue to violet.
     F Calyx with a bulge on upper side, the lips entire, not spiny; fls. 1 per lf.
      Scutellaria tuberosa, p. 145
     FF Calyx without a bulge, the teeth spiny, the upper lip entire or 3-toothed, the lower lip 2-toothed; fls. in 1–sev. whorls (circles). . . . .
      Salvia columbariae, p. 145
    EE Calyx regular, with 5 spiny teeth; fls. rose-pink, in whorls (circles) on stem. . . . . .
     Stachys rigida, p. 146
   DD Perennial with trailing stems; fls. white, 1 per lf. . . . .*Satureja douglasii*, p. 147
  CC Stem round or square; lvs. alternate or opposite, odorless; ovary not lobed, maturing into a dry many-seeded capsule (fr.-pod). (**Scrophulariaceae**)
   D Lvs. opposite (at least the lower ones); without conspicuous bracts beneath flowers.
    E Fls. not yellow.
     F Annual; fls. white, pink, rose to purple, the middle of lower lip enfolding stamens. (*Collinsia*, p. 149)
      G Fls. in sev. whorls (circles). . . . .
      C. heterophylla
      GG Fls. 1 per lf. . . . . . .*C. sparsiflora*
     FF Perennial; lower lip without a fold.

G Fls. maroon; lower lip very short.
  Scrophularia californica, p. 150
GG Fls. blue; lower lip about same
  length as upper lip . . . .
  Penstemon heterophyllus, p. 150
EE Fls. yellow . . . . .*Mimulus guttatus,* p. 151
DD Lvs. alternate; bracts beneath fls. conspicuous,
often colored red, yellow, or white.
  E Perennial; upper lip of corolla long and
  narrow, the lower lip minute.
    F Lvs. simple or few-lobed; fls. yellow to
    scarlet-red.   (*Castilleja*, p. 151)
      G Lvs. not white-woolly.
        H Lower lip of corolla well-hid-
        den within calyx.
          I Hairs on stem and leaves
          harsh, none glandular. .
            1. *C. affinis*
          II Hairs on stem and leaves
          soft, some glandular . .
            2. *C. wightii*
        HH Lower lip of corolla showing
        above the slit in calyx. . . .
          4. *C. franciscana*
      GG Lvs. white-woolly. .3. *C. foliolosa*
    FF Lvs. fern-like; fls. purple-red . . . .
      Pedicularis densiflora, p. 156
  EE Annual; upper lip of corolla short and
  snout-like; lower lip with 3 pouches.
    (*Orthocarpus*, p. 153)
    (*move left for* F)
F Plant small, inconspicuous; fls. ±1/4 in. long, 1 per lf.,
  reddish brown . . . . .1. *O. pusillus*
FF Plant relatively large and conspicuous; fls. 1/2 in. or more
long, in crowded spikes.
  G Fls. mainly white or yellow, their bracts green or often
  white- or yellow-tipped.
    H Stamens longer than upper corolla-lip, showing;
    fls. cream to yellow . . . . .2. *O. floribundus*
    HH Stamens shorter than upper corolla-lip, hidden.
      I Foliage purplish; upper corolla-lip purple;
      lower lip white or yellow. . .3. *O. erianthus*
      II Foliage green; upper corolla-lip not purple.
        J Bracts green; fls. uniformly yellow.
          K Lvs. not hairy. . . .4. *O. faucibarbatus*
          KK Lvs. short-hairy. 5. *O. lithospermoides*

                    JJ Bracts white-tipped; fls. white to yellow
                        (or ± purplish) .....6. *O. attenuatus*
        GG Fls. and bracts pink-lavender to rose-purple.
            H Upper corolla-lip erect, ± hairy. 7. *O. densiflorus*
            HH Upper corolla-lip hooked, densely purple-
                    bearded. ....8. *O. purpurascens*
 **2 Ovary inferior (calyx and corolla attached at top of ovary;
        ovary visible at base of fl.)**
 A Plant with branched tendrils ......*Marah fabaceus*, p. 158
 AA Plant without tendrils.
        B Fls. pale pink, in loose clusters; corolla with a spur at
            base of tube; calyx reduced to a minute ring. ......
                                        Plectritis spp., p. 158
        BB Fls. various colors, in dense heads, each head encircled
            at base by an involucre (1 – sev. rows of green bracts)
            and simulating a single fl.; corolla not spurred; calyx
            hair-like or scale-like (*pappus*) or absent.
                        (**Compositae**) *(move left for* C)
 C All fls. in the head with strap-like, 5-toothed corollas;
        stem with milky juice.
        D Fls. white to pinkish ..*Malacothrix floccifera*. p. 161
        DD Fls. yellow.
            E Heads nodding, closed in fl.; pappus of *ca.* 5 flat
                papery scales each ending in a bristle. ....
                                    Microseris spp., p. 159
            EE Heads open, erect in fl.; pappus of many delicate
                bristles ....*Agoseris* spp., p. 160
 CC At least some of the fls. in the head with tubular, 5-lobed
        corollas; stem with watery juice.
        D Head with tubular (*disk-*) fls. in center and strap-
            like (*ray-*) fls. around edge.   (p. 40 for DD)
            E Ray-fls. white or lavender.
                F Ray-fls. lavender, disk-fls. yellow; head single,
                    large ....*Erigeron glaucus*, p. 162
                FF Ray- and disk-fls. both white; heads small,
                    numerous.
                    G Lvs. ferny. ..*Achillea millefolium*, p. 172
                    GG Lvs. very large, palmately lobed; creek
                            banks in forest. *Petasites palmatus*, p. 173
            EE Ray-fls. yellow or yellow tipped with white.
                F Bracts of involucre each folding around to
                    partly or entirely enclose the ovary (later
                    the fr.) of a ray-fl.   (p. 39 for FF)
                    G Ray-fls. inconspicuous, ± reddish-tipped;
                        pappus of silvery scales, very conspicu-
                        ous in fr. ..*Achyrachaena mollis*, p. 169

GG Ray-fls. conspicuous, not reddish-tipped;
    pappus absent or not as above.
    H Lvs. long and grass-like, very silvery
        hairy; bracts of involucre each but
        half enfolding the fr. of a ray-fl. ...
            Hemizonia multicaulis. p. 165
    HH Lvs. not as above; bracts each com-
        pletely enfolding the fr. of a ray-fl.
        (*Madia*, p. 166 and *Layia*, p. 167)
        I Ray-fls. all yellow.
            J Perennial, the root woody; in
                forests. ...*Madia madioides*
            JJ Annual, the root not woody; in
                woodsy openings or grass-
                land.
                K Lvs. entire or very shal-
                    lowly toothed; stem not
                    spotted. .*Madia elegans*
                KK Lvs. entire to deeply pin-
                    nately lobed; stem with
                    dark spots. ....
                        Layia gaillardioides
        II Ray-fls. yellow tipped with white.
            J Lvs. hairy and ± glandular. ..
                Layia platyglossa
            JJ Lvs. not or only slightly hairy,
                not glandular. ....
                Layia chrysanthemoides
FF Bracts of involucre not folding around ray-fls.
    G Annual, the root not woody.
        H Lvs. opposite.   (*Baeria*, p. 169)
            I Perennial; heads 3/4–1¼ in. wide;
                ocean bluffs. ......*B. macrantha*
            II Annual; heads 1/4–3/4 in. wide;
                widespread. ......*B. chrysostoma*
        HH Lvs. alternate.
            I Lvs. simple, usually entire, woolly;
                involucre cup-shaped, its bracts
                united. ..*Monolopia major*, p. 170
            II Lvs. compound, pinnately dissected.
                J Bracts of involucre in 1 row,
                    united. ....
                        Blennosperma nanum, p. 171
                JJ Bracts in 2 unlike rows, the
                    inner erect, outer spreading.
                        Coreopsis spp., p. 164

[39]

GG Perennial, the root woody.
    H Bracts of involucre white-gummy. . . .
        Grindelia spp., p. 162
    HH Bracts of involucre not as above.
      I Lvs. simple, entire, mostly basal.
        J Lower stem-lvs. opposite. *Heli-
          anthella californica,* p. 164
        JJ Stem-lvs. alternate.
           (*Wyethia,* p. 163)
          K Bracts of involucre lance-
            shaped, to 1+ in. long.
            W. angustifolia
          KK Bracts of involucre ovate,
            some leafy and to 3 in.
            long. . .*W. helenioides*
      II Lvs. toothed or lobed, white-woolly,
        mostly on stem. . . . .
        Eriophyllum lanatum, p. 171
DD Head with tubular (disk-) fls. only.
  E Disk-fls. around margin of head enlarged and with
    unequal lobes. .*Chaenactis tanacetifolia,* p. 172
  EE All disk-fls. alike in head.
    F Lvs. prickly.   (*Cirsium,* p. 175)
      G Stem very low or occas. to 12 in. tall. . .
        C. quercetorum
      GG Stem 1½–3 ft. tall.
        H Bracts of involucre densely cob-
          webby. . . . .*C. occidentale*
        HH Bracts not cobwebby. *C. proteanum*
    FF Lvs. not prickly.
      G Lvs. opposite. .*Arnica discoidea,* p. 175
      GG Lvs. alternate . . . .
      Senecio aronicoides, p. 174

DESCRIPTIVE LIST OF SPRING WILDFLOWERS OF SAN FRANCISCO BAY REGION

LILY FAMILY *Liliàceae*

The Lily Family (tulips, lilies, hyacinths, etc.) has numerous members of horticultural fame, among them many of our spring wildflowers (False Solomon's Seal, Clintonia, fritillaries, Camas, trilliums, etc.), some of which have been grown in European gardens for over

× 1/2

Fig. 1

100 years. Our species are perennials from underground woody or fleshy stems (rootstocks) or from bulbs; flowers mostly showy, the parts in 3's or 6's.

Star Lily or Star Zigadene, fig. 1, pl. 1c

Zigadènus fremóntii (*Zig-adenus,* join and gland, for shape of gland at base of each sepal and petal; *fremontii* commemorates U.S. explorer John C. Fremont).

Among our earliest wildflowers. Flowers in a raceme or panicle, each flower *ca.* 3/4 in. wide, with a lovely star-like pattern. On brushy or wooded slopes the plants are 2–3 ft. tall, chaparral fires favoring their spread and vigor. In grasslands the plants are only 4–10 in. tall (var. *mìnor*). Bulbs of a related species (Z. *venenòsus,* Death Camas) are very poisonous and bulbs of all zigadenes are suspect. Widespread: Bd. Ev. For., Chap., Grass. Feb.–July.

[41]

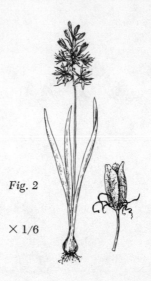

Fig. 2

× 1/6

Camas, fig. 2

Camássia quàmash (both common and scientific names from the Indian name, Camas or Quamash).

A late spring beauty which may color meadows with sheets of blue. The bulbs are very nutritious and were highly esteemed by Indian tribes, but great care had to be used in gathering them because of their strong similarity to the bulbs of Death Camas (a *Zigadenus*, see above). Flowers 3/4–1¼ in. long, in age each of the narrow blue segments coiling separately over the pod. Wet meadows and bogs, Marin and Sonoma Cos.: Fresh. Marsh in Doug. Fir For. and Bd. Ev. For. May–July.

Mariposa Lily, Star Tulip, Globe Lily
Calochórtus

The common names refer to three quite distinct groups in the genus, while *Calo-chortus* refers to the beautiful

[42]

flowers and grass-like leaves. The bulbs were an important food for California Indians.

White Mariposa Lily, fig. 3, pl. 1a

1. *C. venústus* (charming, handsome).

In late spring this and the next species dot the drying hillsides with elegant flowers which are like hovering clusters of white or yellow butterflies. Well-named, in Spanish, *Mariposa* means butterfly.

To 2 or more ft. tall. No two flowers quite alike in color or markings; usually white to lilac, they shade to purple, red, or rarely yellow, with ornate markings around the red blotch on each petal. When yellow-flowered, White Mariposa Lily is hard to tell from Yellow (next species), but the glands at base of each petal are always squarish in White Mariposa Lily. Dry open slopes: Oak Wood., Grass. Apr.–July.

× 1/2

Fig. 3

[43]

Yellow Mariposa Lily

2. *C. lùteus* (yellow, the flowers).

Much like preceding, but flowers always yellow, the glands crescent-shaped. Petal markings very variable, with or without a reddish brown blotch. Dry slopes: Bd. Ev. For., Oak Wood., Grass. Apr.–June.

Star Tulip

3. *C. umbellàtus* (flowers in umbel-like clusters).

The basal leaf of the star tulips (this and next species) overtops the 3–10 in. stem by 2–3 lengths. Flowers white to lilac in this species, only a few hairs around petal-gland. Wooded hillsides, mostly n. of S.F. Bay: Bd. Ev. For., Chap. Feb.–June.

Hairy Star Tulip or Pussy Ears, fig. 4

4. *C. tòlmiei* (named for an early botanist, W. F. Tol-

Fig. 4

× 1/2

mie) [*C. caerùleus* var. *maweànus*].

Like preceding, but flowers rose- or purple-marked, the petals very hairy all over inner surface, hence Pussy Ears. Grassy slopes or in woods, mainly on w. side outer Coast Ranges: Cst. Scr., Redw. For., Pon. Pine For., Bd. Ev. For., Chap. Apr.–June.

White Globe Lily or Fairy Lanterns, fig. 5

5. *C. álbus* (white, the flowers).

A delightful wildflower. Stem 1–2 ft. tall, gracefully branched, each branch with 2–3 delicately fringed, white to rose, nodding flowers 1–1¼ in. long. Woods, Santa Cruz Mts. and w. side Mt. Hamilton Range: Pon. Pine For., Oak Wood., Chap. Apr.–June.

Mt. Diablo Golden Globe Lily or Fairy Lanterns

6. *C. pulchéllus* (pretty, beautiful).

Like *C. albus* but even more beautiful, the flowers a rich lemon-yellow. Wooded areas, only on Mt. Diablo: Oak Wood., Chap. May–June.

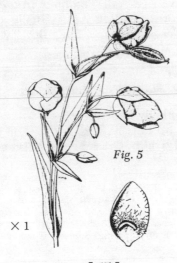

Fig. 5

× 1

Golden Globe Lily or Fairy Lanterns, pl. 1b

7. *C. amàbilis* (lovely).

So much like the preceding that some botanists include both under *C. pulchellus*. Again a very beautiful woodland plant. Marin, Napa, Sonoma Cos.: Pon. Pine For., Bd. Ev. For., Oak Wood., Chap. Apr.–June.

Fritillary   *Fritillària*

Both common and generic names allude to the chessboard-like markings often present on the flowers. Stems arising from bulbs; leaves narrow, often in 1–3 whorls (circles) on stem below flowers; flowers bowl-shaped, usually in a gracefully drooping raceme.

Checker Lily or Mission Bells or Purple Fritillary, pl. 1d

F. lanceolàta (lance-shaped, the leaves).

The most frequent of our fritillaries, the three common names suggested by the somber, bronze-like, often checkered or mottled flowers each 3/4–1 or 1½ in. long. Bulb with tiny "rice-grain" bulblets from which new plants grow; stem 1–2 ft. tall. Usually on wooded slopes: Cst. Scr., Pon. Pine For., Bd. Ev. For., Oak Wood., Chap. Mch.–May.

White or Fragrant Fritillary

F. liliàcea (with lily-like aspect).

Stem 3–12 in. tall; flowers 1/2–3/4 in. long, delicately scented, white. Grassy open hillsides: Cst. Scr. Feb.–Apr.

Very similar to preceding except in odor is the ill-scented Stink Bells *(F. agréstis)* of grainfields in e. part of Bay Region. An unusually showy plant, rare in our area, is Scarlet Fritillary *(F. recúrva* var. *coccínea)*, the flowers brilliant scarlet mottled with yellow; woods of Napa and Sonoma Cos.

Χ 1/1

Fig. 6

False Solomon's Seal   *Smilacìna*

The common name indicates a likeness with the true Solomon's Seal of the Atlantic Coast whose six-pointed flowers resemble the mystic symbol of two intertwined triangles known as Solomon's seal. *Smilacina* (scraper) refers to the stems being rough-hairy in some species. The rootstocks and young leafy shoots were eaten by Indians. Berries red, tasty but cathartic.

Fat Solomon's Seal, fig. 6

S. racemòsa var. *amplexicaùlis (racemosa,* for the flowers in racemes; *amplexi-caulis,* stem-clasping, the leaves).

Stout, to 3 ft. tall; leaves 3–6 in., the bright green foliage making a handsome spectacle on forest floor; stem-tip with a 2–4 in. long panicle of many, small, starry flowers. Shade: Redw.-Doug. Fir For., Bd. Ev. For. Mch.–June.

[47]

Slim Solomon's Seal, fig. 7

S. *stellàta* var. *sessilifòlia* (*stellata,* starry, the flowers; *sessili-folia,* for the stalkless leaves).

Much like preceding, but plants smaller (hence Slim Solomon's Seal) and with usually only 3–9 flowers in a raceme. Shade, brush or trees: Redw.-Doug. Fir For., Bd. Ev. For., Chap. Mch.–June.

Fairy Bells, Fairy Lanterns *Dísporum*

The dainty drooping flowers are the fairy bells or lanterns. *Disporum* alludes to two seeds in each cavity of the ovary. It is another woodland genus, quite similar to *Smilacina* in structure and in habitat.

Fairy Bells, fig. 8

D. hóokeri (for W. J. Hooker, famous English biologist).

To 2 ft. tall; ovate leaves heart-shaped at clasping

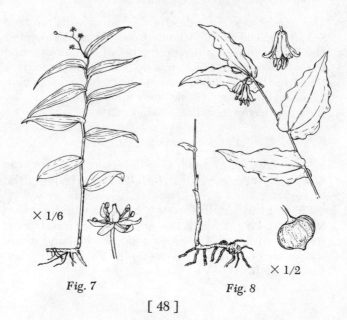

× 1/6

Fig. 7

× 1/2

Fig. 8

base, to 3+ in. long; sepals and petals with tips spreading. Widespread in shady moist woods: Redw.-Doug. Fir For., Bd. Ev. For. Mch.–May.

× 1/8

Fig. 9

Fairy Lanterns, pl. 1e

D. smithii (named for an early English botanist).

To 3 ft. tall; ovate leaves to 4+ in. long; sepals and petals with tips scarcely spreading. Deep shade, coastal: Redw-Doug. Fir For., Bd. Ev. For. Feb.–May.

Closely related to *Disporum* is Twisted-stalk *(Stréptopus amplexifòlius)*, the stems to 3 ft. tall; flowers small, 1 or 2 at base of each leaf. Redw. For. in Santa Cruz Mts. Apr.–May.

Red Clintonia, fig. 9

Clintònia andrewsiàna (genus for De Witt Clinton, eighteenth century statesman; species for T. L. Andrews, first botanist to collect this plant in flower).

[49]

Leaves large, glossy green, basal, always a handsome sight in deep coastal forests; flower-stalk leafless, 10–20 in. tall, with 1–several clusters of small, rosy-red, lily-like flowers, these developing into round blue berries. Redw. For. Apr.–June.

Slink Pod or Fetid Adder's Tongue, fig. 10

Scolìopus bigelòvii (Scolio-pus, crooked foot, for the long sinuous flower-stalk; *bigelovii,* for Dr. J. W. Bigelow, collector on Mexican Boundary Survey, 1850's.)

A fascinating plant, its peculiarities manifest in its common names. The thread-like basal flower-stalks, each ending in a single flower, become very sprawling and sinuous as the 3-angled fruits mature, hence Slink Pods. The flowers, each with petals narrow, erect or incurving, have a foul odor, hence Fetid Adder's Tongue. Stem short, underground, producing 2 broad, glossy, mottled leaves. Deep shade: Redw. For. Jan.–Mch. One of our earliest wildflowers.

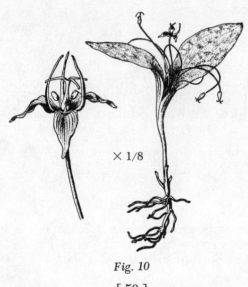

× 1/8

Fig. 10

[50]

Trillium, Wake Robin *Tríllium*

Among the most beloved of woodland wildflowers. *Trillium* alludes to leaves and flower-parts in 3's. Unusual in having 3 broad leaves surmounting an otherwise leafless stem which arises from an underground tuber, in the center of the leaves a single large flower; tubers violently emetic if eaten.

Common or Giant Trillium pl. 1f

T. chloropétalum (refers to the occasional greenish tint of petals) [*T. séssile* var. *gigantèum*].

Stem 10–20 in. tall; leaf-blades 2–5 in. long, green mottled with darker green; flower 2–4 in. long; petals narrow, deep reddish purple or sometimes greenish to whitish. Moist soil, shade: Cst. Scr., Redw.-Doug. Fir For., Bd. Ev. For. Feb.–May.

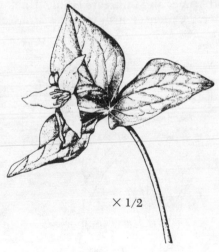

× 1/2

Fig. 11

Coast Trillium or Western Wake Robin, fig. 11

T. ovàtum (in reference to the ovate leaves).

The long-stalked white flower about 1½ in. long makes Coast Trillium very distinct from Common Trillium. Leaves unmottled; petals lanceolate to ovate. Moist shaded forest floor, mainly near coast: Redw.-Doug. Fir For., Bd. Ev. For. Mch.–May.

Another member of the Lily Family, rare in our area, is Two-leaved Solomon's Seal (*Maiánthemum dilatàtum*), like False Solomon's Seal but leaves heart-shaped. Fresh. Marsh near coast.

AMARYLLIS FAMILY *Amaryllidàceae*

Wild Onion *Állium*

Allium is thought to mean either garlic or hot and burning. Regardless of how the name came to be, however, the odor and taste of all onions put them beyond disguise. Both leaves and bulbs are edible. Unlike the well-known Sierra Onion of lush meadows, our onions are

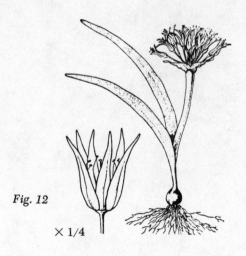

Fig. 12

× 1/4

scattered, mostly in dry areas, often on soils of serpentine rock. Bulbs layered; leaves basal, grass-like, 1–4; flowers in a terminal cluster (umbel), white to deep rose. Eight or nine species occur sparingly in the Bay Region, but only two of these are listed below.

Sickle-leaved Onion, fig. 12

A. falcifòlium (leaves sickle-shaped) [*A. bréweri*].
Known by its short flat flower-stalk, 2 flat curved leaves, and deep rose flowers about 1/2 in. long. Rocky slopes: Bd. Ev. For., Oak Wood., Chap. Apr.–June.

Serrated Onion, fig. 13

A. serràtum (serrated, the markings on bulb-scales.)
Leaves 1–4; pink flowers *ca.* 3/8 in. long. Heavy rocky soil of valleys and slopes, inner Coast Ranges from Solano Co. to Mt. Hamilton Range, also Santa Cruz Mts.: Oak Wood., Chap., Grass. Apr.–May.

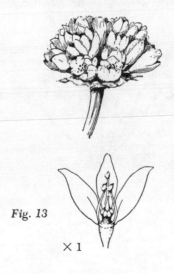

Fig. 13

× 1

Brodiaea   *Brodiaèa*

Brodiaea was named for James Brodie, early Scotch botanist. Like *Allium* in its underground (but solid) bulbs; 1–4 long, narrow, basal leaves and leafless flower-stalk topped by a loose or tight flower-cluster (umbel). A well-known, admired group of spring and early summer wildflowers. Bulbs edible.

White Brodiaea or Wild Hyacinth, fig. 14

1. *B. hyacínthina* (resembling the Hyacinth).
Flower-stalk 1–2 ft. tall; flowers in a loose cluster, white tinged with green; stamens 6, in 1 row. Heavy soil, low wet areas: Fresh. Marsh in Cl. C. Pine For., Oak Wood., Grass. Apr.–June.

Blue Dicks or Common Brodiaea, fig. 15

2. *B. pulchélla* (pretty, beautiful) [*B. capitàta*].
Best known and most common of brodiaeas, its 1/2–2 ft. flower-stalk with a tight cluster of violet-blue

Fig. 14

× 2/3

flowers; stamens 6, in 2 unlike rows. Many habitats: most Bay Region communities. Feb. Apr.

Ookow

3. *B. congésta* (tight, the flower-cluster) [*B. pulchélla* of some authors]. Ookow is the Indian name.

Like Blue Dicks (above), but 3 or more ft. tall, stamens 3, and blooming later. Drying grassy slopes: Bd. Ev. For., Oak Wood. Apr.–June.

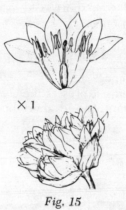

× 1

Fig. 15

Ithuriel's Spear or Grass Nut, pl. 1g

4. *B. láxa* (loose, the flower-cluster).

The angel Ithuriel revealed a disguised Satan by touching him with his own spear (Milton's Paradise Lost); Grass Nut refers to habitat and deeply buried edible bulbs. A variable but always showy beauty. Flower-stalk *ca.* 1–2 ft. tall; flowers to 1½ in., blue-violet, the tips spreading; stamens 6, in 2 rows. Common, flats or slopes, sun or partial shade: Bd. Ev. For., Oak Wood., Grass. Apr.–June.

Several other brodiaeas are noteworthy. Harvest Brodiaea (*B. élegans*), like *B. laxa* but with 3 stamens, starts to bloom on grassy slopes as *B. laxa* reaches its peak. Dwarf Brodiaea (*B. ter-*

réstris) has stalks so short the blue flowers hug the ground; stamens 3; Cst. Scr., Grass. Golden Brodiaea (*B. lùtea*) [*B. ixioides*] has golden-yellow flowers; stamens 6; San Mateo Co.

IRIS FAMILY *Iridàceae*

Sisyrinchium *Sisyrínchium*

Sis-yrinchium comes from pig and snout, on account of swine grubbing at the woody roots. Stems flat, 10–20 in. tall; leaves narrow, grass-like, stiff, folded at base; flowers 3–7 per cluster, short-lived, usually only 1 of a cluster in bloom at once.

Blue-eyed Grass, fig. 16, pl. 1h

S. béllum (handsome).

The common name expresses the charm and habit of this well-known plant. Leaves short, borne on branched

× 1

Fig. 16

[56]

stems; flowers deep blue or violet, yellowish at center. Widespread, often abundant in grassland: most Bay Region communities. Feb.–May.

Golden-eyed Grass

S. califórnicum (of California).

Quite similar to preceding, but leaves long, basal; stems unbranched; flowers yellow. Rare, near coast: Fresh. Marsh. Mch.–May.

Iris   *Iris*

Iris means rainbow, many species being brilliantly colored. Rootstocks heavy and woody; flowers elaborate, the spreading sepals larger and more attractive than the erect petals; styles 3, petal-like. Study a flower and look for the styles, their stigmatic surfaces (the part receiving pollen), and the 3 stamens. Irises may be bafflingly hard to name to species since plants of different species may hybridize with each other to produce progeny with variable-sized flowers of many attractive shades and color-patterns.

Douglas' Iris or Mountain Iris, fig. 17

I. douglasiàna (for David Douglas, the first botanist to collect intensively in California — 1830's).

To 2 ft. tall; flowers deep (or light) blue to red-purple. Forming large colonies on open coastal hills. Also frequent in woods and forests, here the flowers in light and delicate shades of cream to yellow, blue or lavender (var. *màjor*). Cst. Scr., Redw.-Doug. Fir For., Bd. Ev. For., Grass. Feb.–June.

Ground Iris

I. macrosìphon (long-tubed, the flowers).

Low slender stems with small lilac flowers close to

× 3/8

Fig. 17

ground. Open hills or woodsy openings: Redw.-Doug. Fir For., Bd. Ev. For., Oak Wood., Grass. Feb.–June.

Coast Iris

I. longipétala (long-petaled).

To 2 ft. tall; sepals whitish or lilac, veined with violet, yellow-centered; petals violet. In colonies in heavy soil near coast: Cst. Scr., Grass. Mch.–May.

ORCHID FAMILY *Orchidàceae*

Spring-blooming orchids are rare in the Bay Region, but if lucky you may find some. Calypso *(Calýpso bulbòsa)* and Lady's Slipper *(Cypripèdium califórnicum)* are both of deep woods in Marin Co. and n., Calypso with one, Lady's Slipper with a few, large, showy flowers. Rein Orchis *(Habenària unalaschénsis)* is more widespread, with many, small, greenish white flowers in a long spike. Coral Root *(Corallorrhìza maculàta,* pl. 3a, and C. *striàta)* is like Rein Orchis but with the plants brownish, lacking green color, the flowers whitish or pinkish striped or tinged with purple.

Birthwort Family *Aristolochiàceae*

Wild Ginger, fig. 18

Ásarum caudàtum (Asarum, ancient name of obscure origin; *caudatum*, tailed, the 3 perianth segments).

The heavy woody rootstocks are aromatic and the crushed leaves exude a similar pungence, hence Wild Ginger. The rootstocks of the related A. *canadénse* are used as a ginger substitute. Flowers large, long-lasting, well-hidden among the abundant long-stalked, heart-shaped, glossy-green, large and conspicuous leaves. Deep moist soil in dense shade, often carpeting the forest floor: Redw.-Doug. Fir For. Mch.–July.

Fig. 18

× 1/2

× 1/6

[59]

Plants of the Buckwheat Family are mostly summer-
or fall-blooming. Docks, sorrels, cultivated Buckwheat,
wild buckwheat, Rhubarb belong here.

Pink Chorizanthe, pl. 2a

Chorizánthe membranàcea (Chori-zanthe, to divide and
flower, for the 6-lobed perianth; *membranacea,* for the
membrane-like envelope around each flower).

Annual 1/2–1½ ft. tall; herbage gray-woolly; flowers
small, pink, inconspicuous, hidden within pinkish involucres (envelopes), these grouped in tight clusters;
involucres flaring, their 6 slender hooked spines alternating with membranous areas that make a webbing
between the spines. Dry rocky slopes inland: Oak
Wood., Chap., Grass. May–July.

Fig. 19

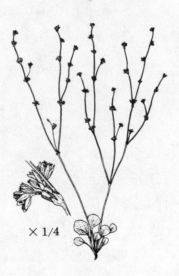

× 1/4

Many kinds of Wild Buckwheat *(Eriógonum)* bloom in summer or fall. One spring-blooming species, however, is *E. covilleànum* (fig. 19), common on shale slopes, Mt. Hamilton Range, Apr.–June. A common summer-blooming species starting to bloom in May is Naked-stem Buckwheat *(E. latifòlium)*, mainly June–Oct.

Four-O'Clock Family *Nyctaginàceae*

Sand Verbena *Abrònia*

Robust prostrate plants of the seashore, the foliage gummy, sand clinging to it; leaves succulent, opposite, those of a pair often unequal in size.

Yellow Sand Verbena, fig. 20, pl. 2b

A. latifòlia (broad-leaved).

Flowers in clusters, bright yellow and fragrant. The roots were eaten as a delicacy by Northwest Indians. Beaches above high tide: Cst. Str. May–Nov.

Pink Sand Verbena

A. umbellàta (flowers in a flat-topped cluster).

Quite similar to preceding, but flowers rose-purple. Beaches above high tide: Cst. Str. Feb.–Nov.

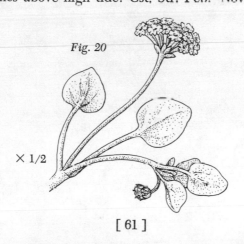

Fig. 20

× 1/2

[61]

7

PURSLANE FAMILY *Portulacàceae*

Red Maids, fig. 21, pl. 2d

Calandrínia ciliàta var. *menzièsii (Calandrinia* for an early Swiss botanist, J. L. Calandrini; *ciliata,* fringed, the sepals with coarse hairs; *menziesii* for Archibald Menzies, first botanist to visit the Pacific Northwest— 1790's) [*C. cauléscens* var. *menzièsii*].

Red Maids aptly designates these lowly annuals of early spring, very inconspicuous until, in full sun, the red-purple petals open wide. The juicy herbage is tasty in salads or cooked as a potherb. The shiny black seeds were ground by Indians to make *pinole.* Often in cultivated fields or orchards; abundant in wet years: Oak Wood., Grass., Rur. Feb.–June.

Fig. 21

× 1

Montia *Móntia*

Named for Joseph Monti, early Italian botanist. Small, somewhat succulent annuals, usually smooth and hairless; leaves in a basal cluster at ground-level, also 2 (or sometimes more) on stem.

Spring Beauty or Small-leaved Montia, fig. 22

M. parvifòlia (small-leaved).

Leaves both basal and alternate on the weak, sprawling stems; small bulblets at base of each stem leaf dropping off to form new plants; petals white to pink, ca. 3/8 in. long. Moss-covered rocks in coastal forests: Redw.-Doug. Fir For., Bd. Ev. For. Apr.–July.

Miner's Lettuce or Indian Lettuce, fig. 23

M. perfoliàta (with leaf surrounding stem).

The numerous, fleshy, basal leaves are good nibbling, the common names deriving from their use as a salad-green or potherb by Indians and early settlers. The erect, otherwise leafless stems are topped by a conspicuous leafy disk (really 2 opposite leaves fused together) which forms a saucer beneath the cluster of small white flowers. Seeds black and shining. Abundant in shade: most communities, sometimes weedy in orchards, etc. Feb.–May.

Fig. 22

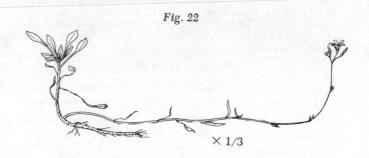

× 1/3

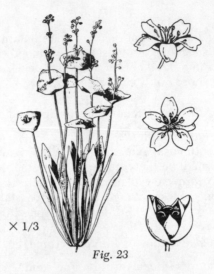

× 1/3

Fig. 23

Common Montia

M. spathulàta (spoon-shaped, the leaves) [*M. gypso-philoìdes*].

A smaller version of Miner's Lettuce, the 2 opposite stem-leaves fused partway or on 1 side only. Herbage often with a whitish or pinkish bloom; flowers white to rich pink, 3/8 in. long. Moist, often rocky slopes: Bd. Ev. For., Oak Wood., Chap., Grass. Jan.–May.

Another Montia, more striking than the three preceding but rare in our area, is Siberian Montia *(M. sibírica)*; stem-leaves 2, not fused, *ca.* 2 in. long; flowers rich rose. Coastal swamps, Santa Cruz Co. n. to Siberia. Mch.–Aug.

Bitterroot, pl. 2e

Lewísia redivìva (Lewisia for Capt. Meriwether Lewis of Lewis and Clark Expedition, who discovered this perennial species in Montana; *rediviva,* "that which lives again," for the unbelievable tenacity with which the uprooted plants cling to life).

This, the state flower of Montana, is a remarkable plant. Named Bitterroot because of the very bitter taste of its heavy starchy roots, necessity made of these roots a valuable food for Northwest Indians. Leaf-rosette lying flat on ground, so also the magnificent white to pink or rose flowers, the leaves and flowers together making a nosegay of great beauty, the flowers opening only in full sun. In cultivation in England as a rock-garden plant since 1826. Rocky ridges or slopes, inner Coast Ranges: Bd, Ev For., Oak Wood. Apr.–June.

Pink Family *Caryophyllàceae*

Leaves opposite; stems swollen at nodes (joints); sepals 5; petals 5; stamens (in our species) 10.

Field Chickweed

Cerástium arvénse L. (*Cerastium,* horn, for the curved capsules; *arvense,* of cultivated fields).

The pretty white flowers, scattered through the vividly green grasslands of the coastal area, focus one's attention upon this otherwise insignificant plant. Stems 5–10 in. tall, weak, matted at base, sticky-hairy, perennial; petals notched, 1/4–1/2 in. long; styles 5. Cst. Scr., Grass. Mch.–May.

Sandwort, fig. 24

Arenària douglásii (*Arenaria,* sand, for the habitat of many species; *douglasii* for David Douglas, intrepid Pacific Coast botanical explorer of the 1830's).

Delicate annual 2–12 in. tall; stem very slender, much branched; leaves needle-like; flowers numerous, scattered on long slender stalks; petals white, *ca.* 1/4 in. long; styles 3. Dry, open, rocky hillsides: many communities. Mar.–June.

Of same habitat and like the above but smaller is California Sandwort (*A. oalifornica*): stems 1–4 in. tall; fls. 1/8 in.

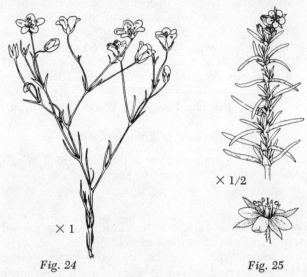

× 1

× 1/2

Fig. 24   *Fig. 25*

Sand Spurry, fig. 25

Spergulària macrothèca (Spergularia, like *Spérgula; macro-theca,* large and box, for the large fruits).

Many small species in this family are called Spurry; this, of sandy areas, is Sand Spurry. Perennial, the stems 4–12 in. tall, sticky-glandular; branches with clusters of small leaves at bases of main leaves; petals pink, 1/4 in. long; styles 3. Coastal: Cst. Str., Cst. Scr., Cst. Salt Marsh. Mch.–Oct.

Indian Pink, pl. 2f

Silène califórnica (Silene, saliva, for Silenus, Greek god who was covered with foam, alluding to the high saponin content which made some of these plants valuable as primitive detergents; species-name apt, for this is the best known of California's pinks).

[66]

This beautiful plant, with its flamboyant scarlet-red petals, is a joy to find. Perennial; stem 1/2–1 ft. tall; leaves to 3½ in., dull green; flowers over 1 in. wide, the petals 4-lobed and again toothed; styles 3. Wooded or brushy slopes: Cst. Scr., Bd. Ev. For., Oak Wood, Chap. Apr.–July.

A very abundant Pink, which masquerades as a native but is in fact a European weed, is Windmill Pink *(Silène gállica)*, with sticky-glandular foliage and small white to pink petals each turned at an angle so that the flower suggests a windmill.

BUTTERCUP FAMILY *Ranunculàceae*

Almost everyone knows the buttercups, columbines, and larkspurs of this family. Perennials with woody roots, palmately compound leaves, 5 often petal-like sepals, 5 or more petals, many stamens and 1–5 or many pistils. The flowers may be irregular, that is, some petals or sepals may differ in shape from others.

Western Baneberry, fig. 26

Actaèa argùta (Actaea, elm, the leaves like elm leaves; *arguta,* sharp, for the toothed leaves) [*A. spicàta* var. *arguta*].

Stem stately, leafy, 1½–3 ft. tall, ending in a column of many delicate, small, white flowers; leaves to 2 ft. long, thrice divided into large, 3-lobed, toothed leaflets; berries 1/2 in. long, shiny red or white, attractive, acrid and poisonous, hence Baneberry. Wooded canyons: Redw.-Doug. Fir For., Bd. Ev. For. Mch.–May.

Columbine, pl. 3b

Aquilègia formòsa var. *truncàta (Aquilegia,* eagle, for the imagined petal-shape; *formosa,* beautiful; *truncata,* truncate, for the short petals). Columbine from *Columbo,* Dove, the flower like a cluster of 5 doves.

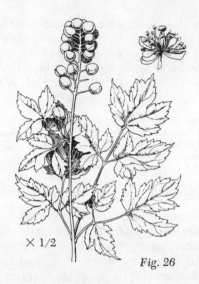

× 1/2

Fig. 26

Widespread but not abundant, an attractive favorite in gardens for at least 100 years and long regarded as a plant of medicinal virtues. The petals are a prominent feature of the elegant flowers, each petal a long hollow tube (nectar-spur) projected backward from stamens. Stem 1½–3 ft. tall, leafy, the leaves with many rounded leaflets; flowers nodding, scarlet, the stamens and petal-bases golden-yellow; pistils 5. Moist wooded or brushy slopes: Bd. Ev. For., Oak Wood., etc. Apr.–June.

Larkspur *Delphínium*

The larkspurs, well-known as garden plants, are represented in the Bay Region by some very beautiful native species which are widely scattered but seldom abundant. Many larkspurs are poisonous, causing disease or death in cattle and horses feeding on them; sheep are seldom affected. Sepals 5, brightly colored, the upper one with a prominent spur; petals 4, small, inconspicuous; stamens many; pistils 3.

[68]

Red Larkspur, fig. 27

1. *D. nudicaùle* (naked and stem, for the few-leaved stem).

This striking species has been in cultivation in England since 1870. Stem to 2 ft. tall, it and leaves hairless; leaves thick, with wide blunt segments; sepals and long spur scarlet-red; petals yellowish. Rocky moist slopes in partial shade: Pon. Pine For., Bd. Ev. For., Oak Wood., Chap. Apr.–June.

Inland Blue Larkspur, fig. 28

2. *D. pàtens* (spreading, for the tips of the 3-parted fruits.) [*D. decòrum* var. *patens*].

Much like Red Larkspur, but with purple-blue flowers which have longer, more widely spreading sepals and a somewhat shorter spur. Moist slopes away from coast, semishade: Oak Wood., Chap. Mch.–May.

Fig. 27

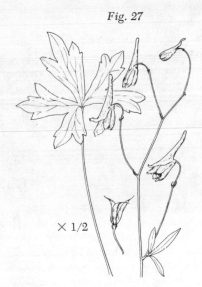

× 1/2

Coast Blue Larkspur

3. *D. decòrum* (elegant, comely).

Much like Inland Blue Larkspur, but not over 8 in. tall, with softly hairy foliage, and usually less than 6 flowers. Grassy coastal slopes: Cst. Scr. Mch.–Apr.

Western Larkspur, fig. 29

4. *D. hespèrium* (of the west).

Stem 1–2 ft. tall, ending in a raceme of greenish blue-purple flowers; leaves with narrow segments, both leaves and stem finely white-hairy. Plants 2–3 ft. tall with whitish to pink flowers are subsp. *palléscens*. Grassy hills or woodsy openings, coming into bloom as the first signs of brown streak the grasslands. Bd. Ev. For., Oak Wood., Grass. May–July.

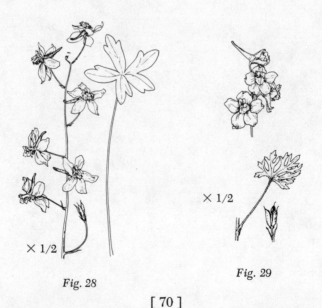

$\times$ 1/2

$\times$ 1/2

Fig. 28

Fig. 29

5. *D. variegàtum* (variegated, probably referring to variable petal-color—whitish, yellowish, blue).

This Larkspur has the largest, most richly colored flowers of any of our species. Flowers 1–1½ in. wide, the sepals a deep royal purple; foliage often coarsely hairy. Grassy or openly wooded hills, mostly inner Coast Ranges: Oak Wood., Grass. Apr.–June.

California Larkspur, pl. 4c

6. *D. califórnicum* (of California).

The largest of our larkspurs, often reaching 6–7 ft.; stem very leafy, topped by a long, dense, often branched raceme of many whitish or dull-purplish flowers; leaves 4–6 in. wide, deeply divided and toothed. Making up in stature for what it lacks in beauty of individual flowers. Wooded or brushy slopes: Bd. Ev. For., Oak Wood., Chap. Apr.–July.

Fig. 30

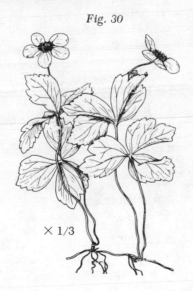

× 1/3

Wood Anemone, fig. 30

Anemòne quinquefòlia var. *gràyi (Anemone,* wind, for
the wind-dispersed fruits; *quinque-folia,* 5-leaved, since
the leaflets may appear to be 5; *grayi,* for Asa Gray,
eminent nineteenth century American botanist).

A delicate woodland plant found in deep shade of
forest floor, usually under redwoods. Stem 4–12 in. tall,
with 3 leaves encircling it just below the one flower,
each leaf divided into 3 toothed leaflets; sepals 5, white
or pale blue; petals 0; pistils many. Redw.-Doug. Fir
For., Bd. Ev. For. Mch.–May.

Meadow Rue, fig. 31

Thalíctrum polycárpum (Thalictrum, to grow green, referring to the bright greenness of young shoots; *polycarpum,* many-fruited, with many fruits per flower).

Meadow Rue comes by its name because the plants
often occur on meadow-margins, the foliage emitting

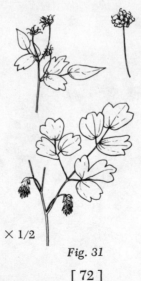

× 1/2

Fig. 31

an unpleasant odor. Although in a family noted for its elaborate floral patterns, Meadow Rue has inconspicuous greenish flowers, the stamens and pistils in separate flowers on different plants, with wind, not insects, as the pollinating agent. Stem 2–3 ft. tall; leaves much-divided. Bd. Ev. For., Oak Wood. Mch.–May.

Buttercup *Ranúnculus*

Many species of *Ranun-culus* (little frog), grow in wet places where frogs abound. The bright yellow flowers (the butter cups) are surely familiar to young and old. The foliage is often somewhat poisonous to livestock. Sepals 5, often colored like petals; petals 5–16; pistils many.

California Buttercup, fig. 32, pl. 2g

R. califórnicus (of California).
Petals lemon-yellow with shiny upper surface, a nectar-gland at base of each petal; pistils maturing into dry

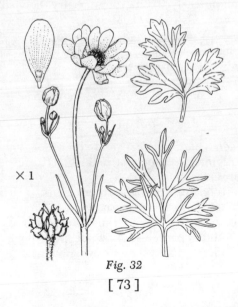

× 1

Fig. 32

one-seeded fruits ("seeds") which were eaten by California Indians. Abundant: many communities. Flowering season long, Feb.–May.

Bloomer's Buttercup

R. bloòmeri (for J. G. Bloomer, early California botanist, first to collect this species).

Stout, somewhat succulent plant 1–1½ ft. tall, usually quite hairless; flowers to 1 or more in. wide, the lemon-yellow petals so shiny as to appear varnished. Similar to but more handsome than California Buttercup, and limited to moist heavy soils of freshwater marshes or low fields, outer Coast Ranges. Feb.–June.

Downy Buttercup

R. hebecárpus (hairy-fruited).

So inconspicuous as to be easily overlooked, this little Buttercup is really quite abundant on moist wooded slopes. Foliage softly hairy; flowers minute, pale yellow; petals falling early; fruits round, hairy, hooked at top. Bd. Ev. For., Oak Wood. Mch.–May.

In ponds, lakes, freshwater marshes, or roadside pools, the white-petaled Water Buttercup *(R. lóbbii)* grows in great masses, its flowers whitening the water's surface.

BARBERRY FAMILY   *Berberidàceae*

Inside-out Flower, fig. 33

Vancouvèria planipétala (genus for Capt. Vancouver, early explorer; *plani-petala*, petals flat, a misnomer as the petals are pouch-shaped) [*V. parviflòra*].

In redwood forests the leathery glossy-green leaves of this plant make a pretty show on the forest floor at any time of year. In spring the delicate leafless flower-stalks produce panicles of small pendulous flowers which, under a hand-lens, show an intriguingly odd

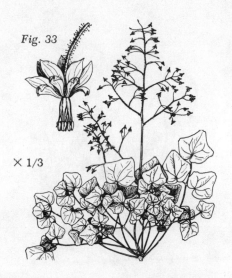

Fig. 33

× 1/3

arrangement, the 6 white sepals and the 6 tiny, orange-lined, white petals turned sharply backward from stamens and pistil. Redw. For. Apr.–Sept.

POPPY FAMILY   *Papaveràceae*

Our four spring wildflowers in this family have much aesthetic appeal and one, the California Poppy, is justly famous. Members of this family often possess at least some of the narcotic properties of the Opium Poppy (*Papàver somníferum*). Annuals or perennials with 2 or 3 sepals which fall very early (look at buds), 4 or 6 petals, many stamens, and 1 pistil.

Cream Cups, fig. 34, pl. 3c

Platystèmon califórnicus (Platy-stemon, broad stamen, for the dilated filaments; *califòrnicus,* of California).

Cream-colored flowers (the cream cups) and softly hairy foliage make of this low plant a charming wild-

Fig. 34

× 1/4

flower, especially pleasing where it grows in abundance among other vernal grassland species. It has been grown in gardens since the 1830's. Stem 3–12 in. tall; leaves entire, opposite; sepals 3; petals 6. Widespread: Oak Wood., Chap., Grass. Mch.–May.

Wind Poppy, fig. 35

Stylomècon heterophýlla (Stylo-mecon, style and poppy, for the style, which is the diagnostic feature of this genus; *heterophylla,* various-leaved, the leaves of many shapes) [*Papàver heterophýllum*].

The Wind Poppy is so-named because its 4, delicate, red-orange petals are very ephemeral, falling when the wind or an unwary hand disturbs them. Stem slender, 1–2 ft. tall, quite hairless; leaves variably toothed or divided. Moist, usually shaded slopes: Oak Wood., Chap., Grass. Apr.–May.

[76]

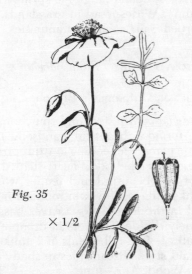

Fig. 35

× 1/2

In Marin Co. the Flame Poppy (*Papàver califórnicum*) replaces Wind Poppy. It is very like Wind Poppy, but with style lacking, the stigma sessile on ovary. Rare except after a fire, then abundant in chaparral or woodland. Apr.–May.

California Poppy, pl. 3d

Eschschòlzia califórnica (genus for J. F. Eschscholz, German physician; species for land of its discovery).

Chamisso, German naturalist who found the California Poppy on San Francisco's sand-dunes in 1816 and named it for his Expedition's surgeon, Eschscholz, could not have guessed that a century later it would be the state flower of California. Well-chosen, too, for in its superb beauty and abundance within the state it has no peers. Early becoming a much-sought garden plant, it now grows as a naturalized "escape" in some countries. California Indians used its narcotic qualities as a pain-killer and ate the leaves as a vegetable. Leaves finely dissected; sepals 2, in bud forming a cap over

[77]

young petals; petals 4, deep orange (in spring) to pale
yellow (in autumn). Widespread in grasslands, occas.
weedy on disturbed soil: many communities. Mch.–
Oct.

FUMITORY FAMILY *Fumariàceae*

Bleeding Heart or Dutchman's Breeches, fig. 36

Dicéntra formòsa (Di-centra, two and spur, some with
2 petals spurred; *formosa,* beautiful, handsome).

Either common name, depending on the observer's
mood, aptly describes the odd, heart-shaped, rose-
purple flowers of this beautiful and tender woodland
plant with fern-like foliage. It was introduced into gardens in England in the late 1700's. Leaves basal, 1 or
more ft. long, finely divided; flowers in drooping clusters on flower-stalks 1–2 ft. tall; petals in 2 unlike pairs,
hiding stamens and style. Streamsides in shady coastal
woods: Riparian Wood. Apr.–June.

Golden Eardrops (*D. chrysántha*) is uncommon but striking;
stem leafy, 2–5 ft. tall; flowers yellow, heart-shaped. Starting to
bloom in May on dry rocky slopes, often in chaparral.

Fig. 36

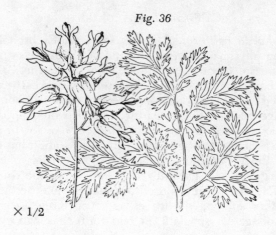

× 1/2

Mustard Family *Cruciferae*

All mustards have a pungent juice, hence the name, Mustard, from musk. Another frequent name for the smaller mustards is Cress. It is a family with many economically important plants (radishes, Brussel sprouts, Cauliflower, Cabbage, etc.). It also includes many of our spring wildflowers and, to the confusion of the neophyte, many introduced (nonnative) spring-blooming weeds as well, some of these weeds now seemingly a natural part of our landscape. Remember, weeds are not dealt with in this book. To tell a Mustard, look for the cruciferous (cross-like) flower-pattern: sepals 4, petals 4, stamens 6 (4 long, 2 short), pistil 1, pod long and narrow (*silique*) or round (*silicle*).

California Mustard, fig. 37

Thelypòdium lasiophýllum (Thely-podium, female and foot, for the stalked ovary; *lasio-phyllum,* hairy-leaved).

Fig. 37

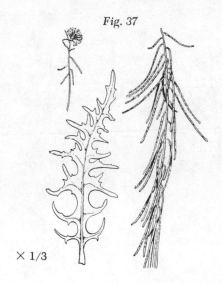

× 1/3

Stem 1–5 ft. tall; leaves sinuately lobed; flowers many, small, whitish; pods 2–4 in. long, reflexed. Widely distributed but only locally common. Open grassy or rocky slopes, often abundant in chaparral after fires: Oak Wood., Chap., Grass. Feb.–May.

Jewel Flower, fig. 38

Streptánthus glandulòsus (Strept-anthus, twisted and flower, for the wavy-margined petals; *glandulosus,* glandular, the teeth of leaf-margin).

The exquisite flowers of the Jewel Flower redeem its coarse herbage. Erect annual 1–2 ft. tall; leaves often roughly hairy and sharply toothed; sepals purplish (whitish in var. *álbidus,* Santa Clara Co.); petals purplish or purple-veined, spreading over sepals. Open rocky slopes, often abundant after fires: Oak Wood., Chap. Apr.–June.

× 1/4

Fig. 38

× 1/2

Fig. 39

Sea Rocket, fig. 39

Cakìle edéntula subsp. *califórnica (Cakile,* old Arabic name; *e-dentula,* without horns or teeth, the pods).

Fleshy-leaved much-branched annual with purplish or white flowers and 2-jointed pods. It grows only on beach sands. The Indians used the roots to make bread and the foliage for salad or potherb. Easily confused with an introduced species also of beach sands, *C. marí-tima,* which has more deeply lobed leaves and pods with 2 horns. Cst. Str. May Nov.

Winter Cress, fig. 40

Barbarèa orthóceras (Barbarea for Santa Barbara; *ortho-ceras,* straight-beaked, the pods) [*B. vulgàris*].

As this Cress may start to grow very early, it is called Winter Cress. Like the well-known, white-flowered, commercially cultivated Water Cress *(Nastúrtium offi-cinàle),* a weed in our area, the leaves of Winter Cress can be used as a salad-green or potherb (Poor Man's

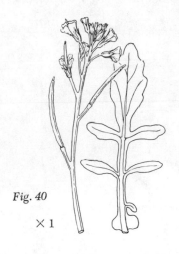

Fig. 40

× 1

Cabbage). Stem 6–18 in. tall; flowers many, small, bright yellow; pods long, erect. Often on disturbed soil or on burns in chaparral, widespread. Moist areas: many communities. Mch.–July.

Bitter Cress, fig. 41

Cardámine oligospérma (*Card-amine*, heart and subdue, for its stomachic value; *oligo-sperma*, few-seeded).

An inconspicuous Cress which, when young, can be eaten as a salad-green. Stem 3–14 in. tall; flowers white. Moist shaded areas, becoming weedy on disturbed ground: Oak Wood., Chap., Urb. Feb.–May.

Milk Maids, fig. 42

Dentària califórnica (*Dentaria*, toothed or horned, for the oddly shaped, tuberous rootstocks; *californica*, of California).

Fig. 41   Fig. 42

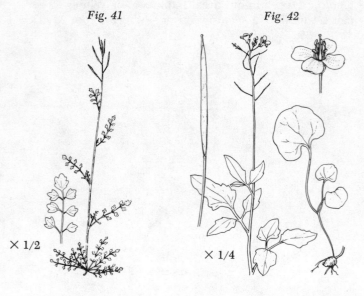

× 1/2   × 1/4

This is one of California's most widespread and characteristic spring wildflowers. Often starting to bloom in winter, its pretty white or faintly pink flowers may continue through April. The swollen rootstocks used to be eaten raw as a peppery relish. Stem to 20 in. tall; leaves somewhat fleshy, hairless, entire or with 3–5 leaflets. Shady woods (var. *califórnica*) or open meadows (var. *integrifòlia*). Redw.-Doug. Fir For., Bd. Ev. For., Oak Wood., Grass. Jan.-Apr.

Rock Cress *Árabis*

The name *Arabis* is derived from Arabia where some of these rock cresses are found.

Tower Mustard, fig. 43

A. glàbra (lacking hairs, the foliage hairless).

An odd-looking tower-shaped plant with little aesthetic appeal. Stem unbranched, 2–4 ft. tall, with numerous

Fig. 43

× 1/4

[83]

leaves progressively smaller upward, the upper ones with ear-like bases; flowers small, white. Occas., many communities. Feb.–May.

Coast Rock Cress, fig. 44, pl. 6c

A. blepharophýlla (fringe-leaved, for the hairy leaf-margins).

Among the earliest of spring wildflowers and very colorful, its 4 petals from deep rose-purple to pink. Stem 4–12 in. tall; leaves with forked hairs fringing the margins. Rocky coastal bluffs and ridges: Cst. Scr., Bd. Ev. For. Feb.–May.

Wallflower   *Erýsimum*

Erysimum, to draw or cure, refers to the reputed medicinal value of the plants. *Erysimum* is known as a wallflower as it sometimes grows on rock-fences or walls. It is an old-fashioned horticultural favorite.

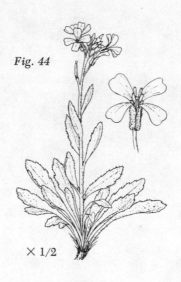

Fig. 44

× 1/2

Common Wallflower, pl. 3e

E. capitàtum (head-like, for the clustered flowers)
[*E. àsperum*].

The bright orange flowers terminating the 1–2 ft. tall,
erect stem make this a handsome plant. Leaves narrow,
irregularly toothed, rough-hairy, grayish green; pods
long, narrow, erect. Usually scattered singly on dry
wooded or rocky slopes, often in disturbed areas: many
communities. Mch.–June.

Franciscan Wallflower

E. franciscànum (of San Francisco).

Much like preceding, but flowers cream or greenish
yellow. Rocky or grassy slopes near coast, Marin to San
Mateo Cos.: Cst. Scr., Chap. Mch.–May.

A replica of *E. franciscanum* but with herbage somewhat fleshy
is *E. concínnum* of maritime headlands, Point Reyes n.

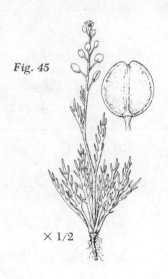

Fig. 45

× 1/2

Common Pepper Grass, fig. 45

Lepídium nítidum (*Lep-idium,* little scale, for the flat round pods; *nitidum,* shining, again the pods).

This tough little plant is very common in grasslands and weedy pastures. The flowers are minute, but soon the shining, disk-shaped, notched pods appear and give Pepper Grass its characteristic aspect. The pods, which turn red-brown with age, are pleasurably peppery to nibble and can be used as a garnish in salads. Open places: Cst. Scr., Chap., Grass. Jan.–Apr.

Dwarf Athysanus, fig. 46

Athýsanus pusíllus (A-thysanus, without fringe, for the wingless pods; *pusillus,* small). No common name.

A delicate plant 4–10 in. tall with a few basal leaves and several sparingly leafy stems bearing minute flowers on recurved thread-like stalks; pods round, somewhat flattened, hairy, forming early. Widely distributed: many communities. Feb.–May.

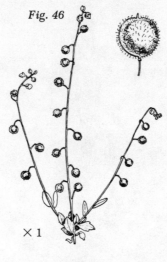

Fig. 46

× 1

[86]

Fringe Pod, fig. 47, pl. 4d

Thysanocárpus cúrvipes (*Thysano-carpus,* fringed fruit, the pods lacy-winged; *curvipes,* curved, the fruit-stalks).

Stem 1–2 ft. tall, its leaves with ear-like bases, the small white flowers in long racemes; pods conspicuous, disk-shaped, somewhat flattened, usually hairy, the pod-margin broad, with many radiating nerves, often perforated between the rays ("windowed"). California Indians ground the pods for *pinole*. Common in grassy areas: Cst. Scr., Oak Wood., Chap., Grass. Mch. May.

STONECROP FAMILY *Crassulàceae*

Broad-leaved Stonecrop, fig. 48

Sèdum spathulifòlium (Sedum, to sit, it often being found on rocks; *spathuli-folium,* for the spoon-shaped leaves).

Stonecrop, so named because it grows gregariously on cliffs, is also known as Hen-and-Chickens from its habit of forming a ring of small flat leaf-rosettes around a large central rosette. Stonecrop is a succulent; its fleshy leaves enhance natural and horticultural rock-gardens at any time of year, but when the multitudes of bright yellow flowers appear in late spring it is especially attractive. The foliage, usually with a whitish bloom, is red-green to purplish on plants growing near the ocean. Maritime headlands or shaded cliffs in coastal forests: Cst. Scr., Redw.-Doug. Fir For., Pon. Pine For., Bd. Ev. For. Apr.–July.

Three other members of this succulent family deserve mention. Sand Pygmy *(Tillaèa erécta)* is a diminutive spring annual present in great quantities in dry sandy or gravelly soil, so small as to be easily overlooked. Rock Lettuce *(Dúdleya cymòsa)* is a conspicuous succulent of rocky ground inland from the immediate coast, Apr.–July. The chalky white leaf-rosettes of Sea Lettuce *(D. farinòsa)* are prominent on ocean bluffs at all seasons, but do not bloom until summer.

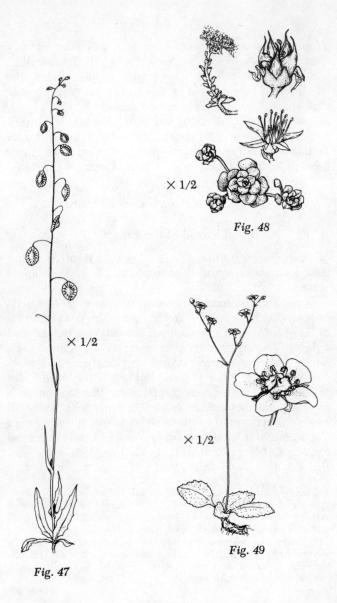

× 1/2

Fig. 48

× 1/2

Fig. 47

× 1/2

Fig. 49

Saxifrage Family *Saxifragàceae*

This is a choice group of small-flowered but beautiful plants growing in moist woodsy areas, the majority of them coming into bloom as spring fades away.

California Saxifrage, fig. 49, pl. 3f

Saxífraga califórnica (*Saxi-fraga*, rock and break, for its reputation as a cure for gallstones) [*S. virginiénsis* var. *californica*].

The small starry flowers with their 5 white petals and 10 red-anthered stamens are gracefully panicled on a leafless stalk 6–10 in. tall. Leaves few, basal, with scattered hairs. Shaded woods, often on mossy rocks or in moist, open, rocky places: Cst. Scr., Cl. C. Pine For., Bd. Ev. For., Oak Wood., Chap. Feb.–Apr.

× 1/2

Fig. 50

Brook Foam, fig. 50

Boykínia elàta (genus for a Dr. Boykin; *elata,* tall).

Often found on stream banks, the large swaying panicles of small white flowers look like so much foam upon the water, hence Brook Foam. Perennial; stem 1–2 ft. tall; leaves round, 1–4 in. wide. Moist coastal woods: Bd. Ev. For., Redw.-Doug. Fir For. May–Aug.

Sugar Scoop, fig. 51

Tiarélla unifoliàta (Tiar-ella, little headdress, for the 2 horns of the pistil which are very unequal in fruit, hence also the fanciful name, Sugar Scoop; *unifoliata,* one-leaved—actually few-leaved).

Stem 1–2 ft. tall, the heart-shaped leaves 1–4 in. wide; flowers small; the petals inconspicuous; stamens long, slender. Moist stream banks of forest floor: Redw. For. May–July.

Fig. 51

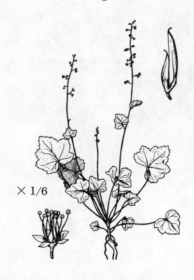

× 1/6

Woodland Star *Lithophrágma*

Litho-phragma, rock and fence, refers to the rock-garden type of habitat, while Woodland Star refers to both habitat and the star-like flowers of these pretty plants. Perennial from small tubers or bulblets; stem erect, unbranched, 1–2 ft. tall; leaves mostly basal, rounded; petals white or faintly pink, showy, lobed on upper half. Two species are common, *L. áffinis* (fig. 52) and *L. heterophýlla;* they are very much alike. To tell them apart, look at flower-base; it is V-shaped in *L. affinis,* U-shaped in *L. heterophylla.* Moist shaded slopes or rocky meadows: many communities. Mch.–June. They may grow together.

Fringe Cups, fig. 53

Tellìma grandiflòra (Tellima, anagram of *Mitella,* a related genus; *grandi-flora,* large-flowered).

Fig. 52

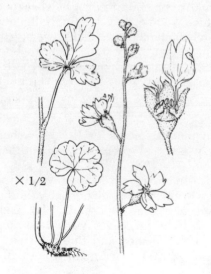

× 1/2

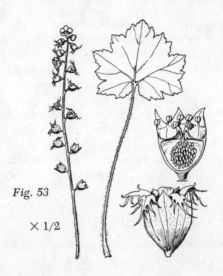

Fig. 53

× 1/2

Fringe Cups earn their name from the deeply fringed petals which arise on the rim of a bowl-shaped green calyx. Rootstock woody; stem 1½–3 ft. tall, ending in a long raceme of many short-stalked flowers; leaves 2–5 in. wide, thin, on long hairy stalks; petals white fading red, 3/8 in. long. Moist wooded areas near coast: Redw.-Doug. Fir For., Bd. Ev. For., Urb. Mch.–June.

Alum Root, fig. 54

Heùchera micrántha (genus for J. H. Heucher, eighteenth century German professor; *micran-tha,* small-flowered).

Alum Root is named from its long woody rootstocks which have astringent and medicinal values. Indians ate the young leaves as a potherb. The plants hang from mossy banks, the leaves very decorative, their hairy blades richly veined and tinted in red. Flower-stem 1–3 ft. tall, with a feathery panicle of small, downy,

white or pinkish flowers. Coastal forests: Cl. C. Pine
For., Redw.-Doug. Fir For., Bd. Ev. For. Apr.–June.

Similar to above, but confined to coastal bluffs and mesas, is
H. pilosíssima, with plants glandular-hairy and the panicle of
flowers condensed. Cst. Scr., Redw. For. Mch.–June.

ROSE FAMILY *Rosàceae*

The large important Rose Family (apples, pears, apri-
cots, plums, strawberries, raspberries, roses, etc.) has
quite a few spring-blooming shrubs and trees in our
area, but only a few herbs which qualify as spring wildflowers. Superficially like the Buttercup Family, the
Rose Family has simple or compound leaves, 5 green
sepals, often 5 bractlets alternating with the sepals,
5 petals, many stamens, and few to many pistils, the
flowers always regular in shape.

Fig. 54

× 1/4

Strawberry *Fragària*

Fragaria, fragrant, for its perfumed berries.

Beach Strawberry, pl. 4a

F. chiloénsis (of Chiloe Island, Chile, where it also grows).

Often used in gardens as a ground-cover; one of the parents of our cultivated strawberry (a hybrid). Its running stems root at the joints to form new plants. The leaflets are 3 per leaf, thick and leathery, silvery green beneath. The large, usually hidden berries are delicious eating. Sand-dunes, ocean bluffs, beaches: Cst. Str., Cst. Scr. Feb.–Aug.

Wood Strawberry, fig. 55

F. califórnica (of California, to which limited).

The Wood Strawberry is more delicate than the preceding, with thinner leaves, smaller flowers, and tiny

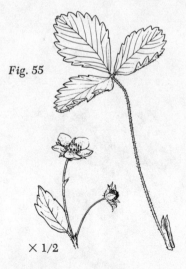

Fig. 55

× 1/2

but flavorful berries. Openly wooded or brushy slopes: Doug. Fir For., Bd. Ev. For., etc. May–July.

Cinquefoil *Potentílla*

Potentilla, powerful, for its reputed medicinal value, much used in earlier times. Many of the yellow-flowered species may be mistaken for buttercups; look for the 5 tiny bractlets between the sepals in *Potentilla*. Cinquefoil (5-fingered) refers to the compound leaves with 5 radiating leaflets in some species.

Sticky Cinquefoil, fig. 56

P. glandulòsa (glandular, the whole plant being sticky and ill-smelling with glandular hairs).

Stem 1–4 ft. tall; leaves with 5–9 leaflets; petals yellow or pale cream; stamens yellow. Widespread, dry hills in woods, brush or grass: many communities. Mch.–July. Sometimes weedy on disturbed soil.

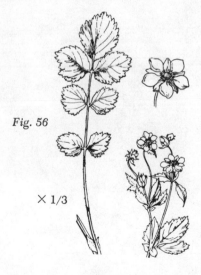

Fig. 56

× 1/3

P. egèdei var. *grándis* (species for Hans Egede of Greenland; *grandis*, large) [*P. anserìna*].

A handsome plant, widespread in swamps along coastlines of Northern Hemisphere. Root edible, tasting like parsnips, a dietary staple for some remote peoples; leaves basal, the bicolored leaflets green above, strikingly silvery beneath, hence Silverweed; flower-stalk leafless, with a single, bright yellow flower; runners rooting at joints to form new plants. Coastal: Cst. Salt Marsh or Fresh. Marsh. Apr.–June.

Pea Family *Leguminòsae*

This huge, economically important family (peas and beans) harbors many of California's wildflowers–lupines, clovers, peas, vetches, trefoils, etc., all of which have alternate, pinnately or palmately compound leaves

Fig. 57

× 1/3

a. *Calochortus venustus*

b. *Calochortus amabilis*

c. *Zigadenus fremontii*

d. *Fritillaria lanceolata*

e. *Disporum smithii*

f. *Trillium chloropetalum*

g. *Brodiaea laxa*

h. *Sisyrinchium bellum*

Plate 1

a. *Chorizanthe membranacea*

b. *Abronia latifolia*

c. *Armeria maritima* var. *californica*

d. *Calandrinia ciliata* var. *menziesii*

e. *Lewisia rediviva*

f. *Silene californica*

g. *Ranunculus californicus*

Plate 2

a. *Corallorrhiza maculata*

b. *Aquilegia formosa* var. *truncata*

c. *Platystemon californicus*

d. *Eschscholzia californica*

e. *Erysimum capitatum*

f. *Saxifraga californica*

g. *Baeria chrysostoma*

Plate 3

a. *Fragaria chiloensis*

b. *Trifolium variegatum*

c. *Delphinium californicum*

d. *Thysanocarpus curvipes*

e. *Lotus humistratus*

f. *Oxalis oregana*

g. *Limnanthes douglasii*
Plate 4

a. *Mentzelia lindleyi*

b. *Epilobium franciscanum*

c. *Lupinus densiflorus*

d. *Clarkia unguiculata*

e. *Oenothera ovata*

f. *Dodecatheon hendersonii*

g. *Clarkia amoena*
Plate 5

a. *Convolvulus soldanella*

b. *Linanthus androsaceus*

c. *Nemophila menziesii* (blue)
with *Arabis blepharophylla* (pink)

d. *Phacelia californica*

e. *Sanicula arctopoides*

f. *Collinsia heterophylla*

g. *Heracleum lanatum* (white)

Plate 6

a. *Amsinckia eastwoodiae*   b. *Castilleja affinis*

c. *Penstemon heterophyllus*   d. *Mimulus guttatus*

e. *Orthocarpus erianthus*

f. *Castilleja franciscana*   g. *Orthocarpus purpurascens*

Plate 7

a. *Erigeron glaucus*

b. *Wyethia helenioides*

d. *Helianthella californica*

c. *Orthocarpus densiflorus*

e. *Layia platyglossa*

f. *Achyrachaena mollis*

g. *Monolopia major*

h. *Cirsium occidentale*

Plate 8

and flowers shaped like sweet peas (5-lobed calyx, 5-petaled corolla with an upper *banner*, 2 side *wings*, and 2 bottom petals fused to form a *keel*, 10 stamens with all filaments united or 1 free), and a fruit which is a 2-valved pod (*legume*).

Fig. 58

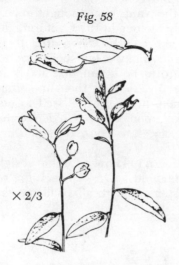

× 2/3

Apt to be looked for in the Pea Family is Milkwort (*Polýgala califórnica,* fig. 58) of the Polygala Family (Polygalàceae): perennial; stems many, 3–10 in. tall, with milky juice; leaves simple; petals 3, rose-purple, irregular, united at base and enclosing 8 stamens. Wooded or brushy areas, outer Coast Ranges. Mch.–July.

False Lupine, fig. 59

Thermópsis macrophýlla (Therm-opsis, lupine-like, like the related *Lupinus; macro-phylla,* large-leaved).

These striking plants can be told at once from true lupines (below) by their leaves which consist of only 3 palmate leaflets, not 4–many. Perennial, stem to 2½ ft. tall; leaflets 1–3 in. long, broad, silky hairy; flowers many, *ca.* 3/4 in. long, bright yellow. Dry open slopes, often in colonies: Oak Wood., Chap., etc. Mch.–July.

Lupine *Lupìnus*

Both common and generic names come from the word *lupus* (wolf), the plants once thought to be destructive (of soil). Justly famous in the California flora, lupines are abundant and colorful. Soon after their discovery by early explorers, many of our species were introduced into horticulture in both America and Europe. Their roots grow deeply, making them important as sand-binders. As such, lupines were used to help stabilize the sand-dunes upon which Golden Gate Park was built. Some species are poisonous, causing disease in stock.

It is easy to learn to know a Lupine at sight (all have palmately compound leaves, flowers in a raceme, a 2-lipped calyx, stamens with all 10 filaments fused, and

Fig. 59

× 1/3

a flattened pod with 2–12 seeds), but it is not so easy to tell one Lupine from another. Some of our most magnificent species are shrubs, but only the more common, nonwoody, spring-flowering ones are given below. Unhappily not all have common names which are truly colloquial.

Intermediate Platycarpos, fig. 60

1. *L. subvéxus* (inclining upward, the banner). Intermediate Platycarpos refers to the flat pods; this is an example of a "coined," noncolloquial common name.

Annual 8–16 in. tall, silky-hairy; flowers 1/2 in. long, first spreading, later erect, blue to red-purple. Hills, valleys: Oak Wood., Grass. Apr.–June.

Gully Lupine, pl. 5c

2. *L. densiflòrus* (dense-flowered) [*L. microcárpus* var. *densiflorus*].

Quite like the preceding but larger, less hairy, the petals whitish to yellow (or tinged bluish or rose). Most

Fig. 60

× 1/2

distinctive are the twisted flower-stalks which bring flowers and pods of each whorl all to the same side of stem. Hill slopes and gullies in grassy openings: Oak Wood., Grass., etc. Apr.–Aug.

Succulent Lupine, fig. 61

3. *L. succuléntus* (succulent, fleshy).

Annual 8–24 in. tall, sparsely hairy; stem stout, often hollow; flowers 1/2 in. or more long, light to deep blue, the banner with a yellow center turning violet in age. Open slopes or valleys or along water-courses: many communities. Apr.–June.

Sky Lupine, fig. 62

4. *L. nànus* (dwarf).

The common name reflects the beauty of the flowers which may form a low canopy of blue over the grasslands. Annual 8–24 in. tall, slender-stemmed and with

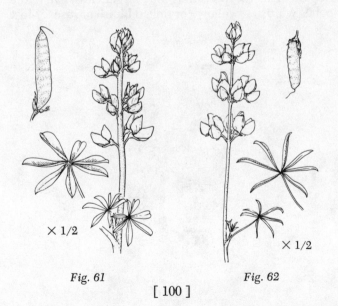

× 1/2   × 1/2

Fig. 61   *Fig. 62*

[100]

narrow leaflets, yet far from dwarf. Flowers much as in *L. succulentus, ca.* 1/2 in. long, violet-blue, the banner with a white or yellow center turning red in age. Grasslands or sandy areas, valleys or hills: Cst. Scr., Oak Wood., Grass. Mch.–May.

Annual or Dove Lupine

5. *L. bìcolor* (2-colored, the petals).

A smaller version of *L. nanus,* often growing with it. Annual 4–16 in. tall, softly hairy, flowers few, *ca.* 3/8 in. long, blue, the broad banner with a white center turning violet, the keel slender and upturned. Sandy open areas, often on disturbed soil: Oak Wood., Grass., etc. Mch.–May.

Very like *L. bicolor* and also widespread is *L. micránthus,* its flowers with narrow banner and short blunt keel. Mch.–May.

Swamp Lupine, fig. 63

6. *L. polyphýllus* (many-leaved) [*L. grandifòlius*].

Fig. 63

× 1/9

The species name of this regal plant reflects an out-standing attribute—its magnificent foliage. Perennial 3–5 ft. tall; leaflets 4–8 in. on stalks 1 ft. long; flowers over 1/2 in., blue to purplish. Marshes and lagoons near coast. Apr.–June.

Broad-leaved Lupine

7. *L. latifòlius* (broad-leaved) [*L. rivulàris*].
Smaller than Swamp Lupine, but still an imposing plant. Perennial 2–4 ft. tall; leaflets to 4 in. on stalks to 8 in. long; flowers over 1/2 in. long, blue to purplish. Brushy or openly wooded areas: many communities. Mch.–May.

Two other lupines deserve mention. Summer Lupine (*L. for-mòsus*) has silvery green mats of foliage and long stalks of large rich blue flowers; gregarious, often in rocky areas. Dec.–Aug. Varied Lupine (*L. variicolor*) is like the preceding in its mats of silvery foliage, the larger flowers white, pink, yellow, or blue with a paler banner; coastal grasslands. Mch.–June.

Fig. 64

× 1/4

Clover *Trifòlium*

Although not so colorful and showy as lupines, clovers are a large, easily recognized and abundant group of wildflowers. Of high nutritional content and important as stock food, they were sought in early spring by California Indians who ate the tender young foliage raw or boiled. *Trifolium* refers to the 3 leaflets per leaf, these always toothed. Flowers small, in heads, the heads often with a green disk of free or united bracts *(involucre)* at base. Only some of the more common species are listed here.

Sour or Bull Clover, fig. 64

1. *T. fucàtum* (painted, for the flower-colors).

Sour Clover is a misnomer, as the herbage is sweet and makes a good salad. Stems stout, hollow, to over 2 ft. long; petals greenish white or cream or tinged light pink, puffily inflated in age. Heavy soils, often on roadsides: many communities. Apr.–June.

Fig. 65

× 1/2

Tomcat Clover, fig. 65

2. *T. tridentàtum* (3-toothed, the calyx lobes).

Stem 4–20 in. tall; leaflets narrow, 1/2–1½ in. long; flowers *ca.* 1/2 in. long; calyx-lobes often toothed on each side of the sharp tip; petals purplish, often white-tipped. Common, grasslands, hills, disturbed areas: many communities. Mch.–June.

White-tip Clover, pl. 4b

3. *T. variegàtum* (variegated, for the splotched leaves).

Stem 1/2–2 ft. tall; leaflets 1/4–1/2 in. wide, 1/2–3/4 in. long; flowers 1/4–3/8 in. long; calyx-lobes gradually narrowed to a point; petals purple, white-tipped. Low areas: many communities. Mch.–June.

Cow Clover

4. *T. wormskjóldii* (for Morten Wormskjold, who first collected it) [*T. involucràtum; T. fimbriàtum*].

Stems thick, weak, 4–24 in. tall; leaflets small; heads large (1–1½ in. wide), of showy rose-red flowers. Marshes, moist coastal bluffs or sand-dunes: Cst. Str., Cst. Scr., Grass., etc. Apr.–June.

Indian or Rancheria Clover, fig. 66

5. *T. albopurpùreum* (white and purple, the flowers).

Quite different from preceding clovers in lacking a disk (involucre) below flower-head. Stem slender, to 16 in. tall; petals purple, sometimes white-tipped, about as long as the narrow, long-hairy calyx-lobes. Perhaps the most abundant and widespread clover in California: many communities. Mch.–June.

Another Indian Clover is *T. dichótomum*, like *T. albopurpureum* but petals longer than calyx-lobes. Also common is small-headed Maiden Clover *(T. microcéphalum)* with light pink flowers.

Trefoil *Lòtus*

Lotus is a Greek name for various plants. Trefoil refers to the leaves, some with only 3 leaflets. Ours are mostly lowly plants found in great numbers in spring, often on disturbed soil and acting as weeds. All have small, mostly yellow flowers and 4–9 or occas. only 3, smooth-margined, pinnate leaflets per leaf.

Witch's Teeth or Coast Trefoil, fig. 67

1. *L. formosissimus* (most beautiful).

Our most attractive Trefoil. Witch's Teeth refers to the long narrow calyx-lobes. Stems prostrate, hairless; leaflets 5–7 or occas. 9; petals 1/2 or more in. long, the banner bright yellow, the wings and keel white to pink or purplish. Low wet soil near coast: Cst. Scr., Grass., etc. Mch.–July.

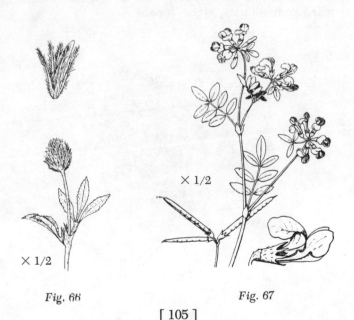

× 1/2

× 1/2

Fig. 66　　　　　　　　　　Fig. 67

Similar in habit to above but with petals uniformly yellow is Bird's Foot Trefoil (*L. corniculàtus*), a European weed becoming common along roads and in fields especially near coast.

Hill Lotus or Small-flowered Trefoil, fig. 68

2. *L. micránthus* (small-flowered).

Though inconspicuous, this is our most widespread and abundant Trefoil. Stems wiry, erect, 3–12 in. tall; foliage hairless; leaflets 3–5; flowers 1/8–3/16 in. long, creamy pink fading red. Grassy or brushy places: many communities. Mch.–June.

Colchita or Short-pod Trefoil, pl. 4e

3. *L. humistràtus* (spread out, prostrate). *Colchita*, little counterpane, also refers to prostrate habit.

Almost as abundant as Hill Lotus. Forming softly silky mats 3–14 in. wide; leaflets usually 4; flowers 1/4 in. long, bright yellow fading red. Drying hills or flats: many communities. Mch.–June.

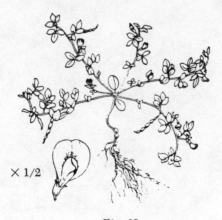

× 1/2

Fig. 68

Calf Lotus or Chile Trefoil

4. *L. subpinnàtus* (somewhat pinnate, the leaflets).
Much like Colchita, but foliage less silky and calyx-lobes shorter. Warm slopes and flats, often with Colchita. Mch.–June. Also in Chile.

Spanish Clover, fig. 69

5. *L. purshiànus* (for F. T. Pursh, early American botanist) [*L. americànus*]. Not a true clover.
Stems usually erect, 6–18 in. tall; foliage somewhat silky; leaflets 4–5; flowers long-stalked, 1/4 in. long, whitish to pink. Common on grassy slopes or in shaded woods: many communities. Apr.–Oct.

California Tea, fig. 70

Psoràlea physòdes (*Psoralea*, scurfy, often with wart-like glands; *physodes*, bladder-like, the calyx).

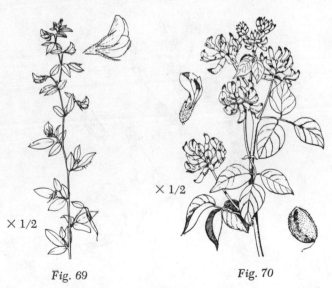

$\times$ 1/2

$\times$ 1/2

Fig. 69   *Fig. 70*

[107]

The gland-dotted herbage of this aromatic plant makes a fair substitute for tea and was so used by pioneers. Rootstock woody; stem erect, to 2 ft. tall; leaflets 3, 1–2 in. long; flowers 1/2 in. long; calyx heavily glandular; petals greenish white to purplish. Woods or brush: Oak Wood., Chap. Mch.–July.

Dwarf Locoweed, fig. 71

Astrágalus gambeliànus (*Astragalus,* vertebra, for the squarish seeds; species for Wm. Gambel, ornithologist and early transcontinental explorer) [*A. nigréscens*].

Locoweeds are so-called since many cause loco disease in stock feeding on them. Annual 2–12 in. tall, often black-hairy; leaflets 7–13; flowers 4–15, small, whitish to violet; pods hairy, wrinkled, bent down. Open hills: Cst. Scr., Oak Wood., Grass. Mch.–May.

Close to the above is another Dwarf Locoweed (*A. didymocárpus)* of e. Contra Costa Co., pods erect instead of bent down.

× 1/2

Fig. 71

[108]

American Vetch, fig. 72

Vícia americàna (Vicia, to bind together, since it climbs by tendrils on other plants; *americana,* of America).

Vetches are very close to peas (*Lathyrus,* next genus); look at style to distinguish them (refer to Key, p. 32). Perennial climbing by tendrils; leaves variably shaped, the leaflets 1/2–1½ in. long; flowers 4–8 per stalk, purplish fading bluish, 1/2–3/4 in. long. Common in grassy or brushy areas or woods: many communities. Mch.–June.

Hillside Pea, fig. 73

Láthyrus vestìtus (Lathyrus, of uncertain meaning; *vestitus,* clothed, as with hairs, hairy).

This common Pea is a close relative of the Sweet Pea (*L. odoràtus*) of horticulture and is also much like Vetch (*Vicia,* above). Variable, blooming very early, the stem angled, low or climbing by tendrils to 3 ft.; leaflets 6–12, 1/2–1 in. long, gray-green, hairy; flowers many per raceme, dull white to pinkish. Wooded or brushy hills: many communities. Feb.–May.

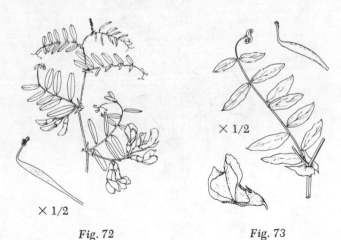

× 1/2

× 1/2

Fig. 72   *Fig. 73*

[109]

Very like Hillside Pea is Buff Pea (*L. jepsònii* subsp. *califórnicus*), but with stem winged, not merely angled. Brushy slopes. Redwood Pea (*L. tórreyi*) is a delicate, fragrant, little-known Pea of coastal forests, its stems 4–10 in. tall, the tendrils rudimentary, the flowers 1–2 per stalk. Redw.-Doug. Fir For., Bd. Ev. For. Apr.–June.

Wood Sorrel Family *Oxalidàceae*

Redwood Sorrel, fig. 74, pl. 4f

Óxalis oregàna (Oxalis, acid, the juice; *oregana,* of Oregon, where discovered by Thomas Nuttall in 1834).

The sour clover-like leaves of this attractive plant make pleasant nibbling and can be added sparingly to salads. Rootstock woody; leaves basal, on 4–7 in. stalks, with 3 heart-shaped leaflets which fold up at night; flower-stalk with 1 large pink to lavender flower. Deep shade, a characteristic ground-cover in Redw.-Doug. Fir For. Feb.–Sept.

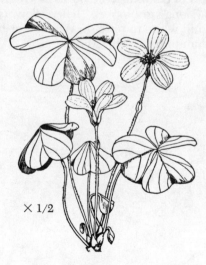

× 1/2

Fig. 74

MEADOW FOAM FAMILY *Limnanthàceae*

Meadow Foam, fig. 75, pl. 4g

Limnánthes douglásii (*Limn-anthes,* marsh and flower, for habitat and habit; *douglasii* for David Douglas, famous Scotch explorer, in California from 1830–1832).

× 3/4

Fig. 75

Meadow Foam, which blooms in profusion on wet low ground, is well-named. Annual; stems 6–18 in. long; leaves yellow-green, smooth, fleshy; flowers showy, the 5 petals 1/2–5/8 in. long, white with yellow centers. Moist flats: Oak Wood., Grass. Mch.–May.

MALLOW FAMILY *Malvàceae*

Checker Bloom or Wild Hollyhock, fig. 76

Sidálcea malvaeflòra (Sidalcea, like *Sìda,* another Mallow; *malvae-flora,* mallow-flowered).

[111]

In springtime grassy slopes are checkered abundantly with the rosy hollyhock-like flowers of Checker Bloom. Some plants have large, light pink flowers which contain both stamens and pistil, while other plants have smaller rose flowers which lack stamens. Perennial 1–2 ft. tall; herbage downy hairy. Coastal mesas and inland: Cst. Scr., Grass. Feb.–June.

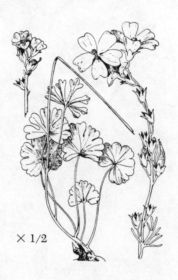

× 1/2

Fig. 76

Less abundant is the annual Fringed Sidalcea (*S. diploscỳpha*) with rose-pink flowers. Apr.–May.

VIOLET FAMILY *Violàceae*

Violet *Vìola*

Viola is the classical name for this widespread group of plants, the name Violet derived from *Viola*. The fragrant flowers may be candied and eaten as a confection.

Redwood Violet, fig. 77

1. *V. sempervìrens* (evergreen) [*V. sarmentòsa*].
Creeping stems with heart-shaped evergreen leaves; flowers 1 to a stalk 2–4 in. tall; petals lemon-yellow, 3/8–1/2 in. long. Deep forests, mostly under redwoods: Cl. C. Pine For., Redw.-Doug. Fir For., Bd. Ev. For. Jan.–Aug.

Stream Violet, fig. 78

2. *V. glabélla* (smooth, for the hairless foliage).
Another yellow-flowered forest dweller with heart-shaped leaves, but stems erect, 4–12 in. tall; leaf-blades 1½–3½ in. long on stalks 3–7 in. long. Riparian Wood. in Redw.-Doug. Fir For., Pon. Pine For., Bd. Ev. For. Mch.–July.

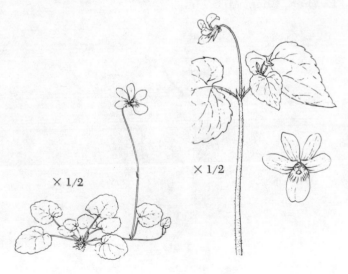

× 1/2

× 1/2

Fig. 77   Fig. 78

Johnny-jump-up or Yellow Pansy, fig. 79

3. *V. pedunculàta* (peduncled, for the stalked flowers).

A favorite of children, who play games with the monkey-faced flowers. Root woody; stem 4–14 in. tall; leaves 1–2 in. long on stalks 1–3 in.; flower-stalks 4–6 in. long, each with a golden-yellow brown-streaked flower *ca.* 3/4 in. long. Open grassy hills: Cst. Scr., Oak Wood., Grass. Feb.–Apr.

Western Heart's Ease or Two-eyed Violet

4. *V. ocellàta* (small-eyed, two of the petals spotted).

Stem erect, 5–12 in. tall; flowers several to a leafy stem; upper 2 petals white inside, purple outside, lower 3 petals white or yellow, the 2 side ones purple-spotted (eyed). Shade or semishade: Redw.-Doug. Fir For., Bd. Ev. For., Chap. Mch.–June.

× 1/4

Fig. 79

Western Dog Violet or Blue Violet

5. *V. adúnca* (hooked, the flower-stalk bent at tip).

Forming low leafy mounds 2–4 in. tall, the light blue to purple flowers on stalks which surpass the ovate leaves. Grassland or meadowy forest openings near coast: Cst. Str., Cst. Scr., Bd. Ev. For., etc. Feb.–Apr.

Loasa Family *Loasàceae*

Golden Blazing Star, fig. 80, pl. 5a

Mentzèlia líndleyi (C. Mentzel, seventeenth century German botanist; John Lindley, nineteenth century English botanist).

The magnificent flowers of this plant long ago earned it a place in gardens. Annual; stem white, 1/2–2 ft. tall; leaves harshly hairy; petals 5, 1+ in. long, golden-yellow with orange-red base; stamens many. Dry, rocky, inland hills: Oak Wood., Chap. Mch.–July.

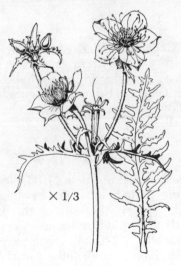

× 1/3

Fig. 80

Golden Blazing Star, above, is not to be confused with the summer-blooming Blazing Star (*M. laevicaùlis*), 2–3 ft. tall, with light yellow flowers 3–4 in. across.

Evening Primrose Family *Onagràceae*

An easily recognized family–sepals and petals 4; stamens 4 or 8; ovary below other flower-parts. Some kinds open their flowers at dusk, most are diurnal.

San Francisco Willow Herb, pl. 5b

Epilòbium franciscànum (Epi-lobium, upon a lobe, for the inferior ovary; *franciscanum,* of San Francisco).

One of our several willow herbs, all of which have erect stems, many willow-like leaves, and smallish flowers. Perennial; herbage reddish; stem 1/2–3 ft. tall; leaves 1–2½ in. long; petals red-purple, deeply notched; pods 2–3 in. long; seeds white-cottony. Fresh. Marsh along coast. Apr.–June.

Clarkia *Clárkia*

Clarkias (for Capt. Wm. Clark of the Lewis and Clark Expedition) are well-known in gardens. A huge series of cultivars has been developed by hybridization, in which Elegant Clarkia (below) has figured importantly. Annuals; flowers showy, pink to purple; stamens 8, 4 of them small.

Elegant Clarkia, pl. 5d

C. unguiculàta (clawed, the petals) [*C. élegans*].

In late spring drying slopes are brightened by the oddly colored, spidery blossoms of this Clarkia. Its nutritious seeds were used by Indians to make *pinole*. Stem white, smooth, 1–3 ft. tall; sepals purplish; petals pink to lavender, long-clawed; anthers scarlet. N.-facing slopes: Oak Wood., Chap., Grass. Apr.–Aug.

Red Ribbons or Lovely Clarkia, fig. 81

C. concinna (neat, well-made, elegant).

Another late spring species, the flowers of bizarre beauty. Stem reddish, 1/2–2 ft. tall; sepals red; petals rose-pink, 1/2–1 in. long, deeply 3-lobed (the red ribbons), 3 pointed up, 1 pointed down; stamens 4. Semi-shade, mostly wooded slopes: Doug. Fir For., Bd. Ev. For., Oak Wood., Grass. May–June.

Starting to bloom in abundance on drying grassy hills in late spring are other Clarkias, formerly of the genus *Godetia,* with petals broad and rounded above, fan-shaped, not clawed. Some of these, known generally as Farewell-to-spring, are *C. gracilis* (fig. 82), petals lavender; *C. amoena* (pl. 5g), also called Summer's Darling, the petals pink or lavender splotched or pencilled with red; *C. purpurea*, petals purplish.

Sun Cup, Evening Primrose   *Oenothèra*

Oeno-thera means wine and catching, the roots once used as incentives to wine drinking. Petals 4, yellow,

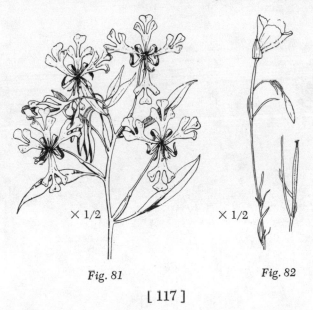

× 1/2   × 1/2

Fig. 81   *Fig. 82*

curving to form a shallow cup (the sun cup); stamens 8. Mostly diurnal, only a few blooming at dusk.

Sun Cup or Golden Eggs, pl. 5e

1. *O. ovàta* (ovate, the leaf shape).

Leaves in a basal rosette 1/2–1 ft. across, wavy-margined, acceptable when young as a salad-green; ovary of each flower buried among leaves, a slender tube 3–4 in. long between it and other flower-parts; petals making a clear yellow cup 1 in. wide. Grassy open areas near coast: Cst. Scr., Grass. Feb.–June.

Dune Sun Cup or Beach Evening Primrose, fig. 83

2. *O. cheiranthifòlia* (leaves like *Cheiránthus*, a Wall-flower) [*O. spirális*].

Stems 1–2 ft. long, prostrate, radiating from a leaf-rosette 1–3 in. wide; leaves thick, white-hairy, 1/2–2 in. long; petals 1/4–1/2 in. long; pods thick, coiled. Beach sands. Cst. Str. Apr.–July.

× 1/2

Fig. 83

Small Sun Cup, fig. 84

3. *O. micrántha* (small-flowered).

Stem 1/2–2 ft. tall, branching, with many wavy-margined leaves; petals 1/8–1/4 in. long; pods sharply 4-angled, coiled. Variable and of many habitats—sand-dunes, sandy fields, rocky slopes, orchards: Cst. Str., Chap., etc. Mch.–June.

Contorted Sun Cup, fig. 85

4. *O. contórta* (contorted, the pods often curved).

More diminutive than preceding. Stems diffuse, slender, 4–12 in. tall; leaves 1/2–1½ in. long, almost hairless; petals 1/8–3/16 in. long; pods cylindrical, straight or curved at base. Sand-dunes to dry ground inland: many communities. Mch.–June.

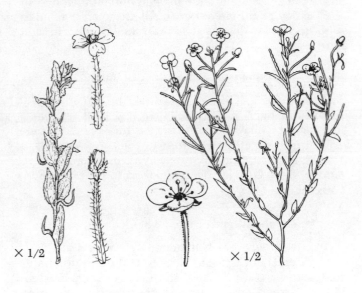

× 1/2   × 1/2

Fig. 84   Fig. 85

[119]

This huge family is known by such market-place and pharmaceutical items as Parsley, carrots, parsnips, Chervil, Anise, Dill, Fennel, Caraway, etc. Many kinds are edible, some aromatic, some very poisonous. All have hollow ribbed stems, divided leaves, and many small flowers in stalked clusters (umbels), each flower with 5 minute or absent sepals, 5 small petals, 5 stamens, and an inferior ovary. Ripe fruits are usually needed to tell one from another. Only the commoner spring-blooming species of our area are given below.

Sanicle or Snake Root *Sanicula*

Sanicula (to heal) and both common names are based on the medicinal properties and reputed value for snake-bite. Sanicles are the most abundant members of the Parsley Family in our area. All are small perennials with smooth few-leaved stems and small flowers in tight clusters.

Footsteps of Spring, pl. 6e

1. *S. arctopoìdes* (like a bear's foot, the leaf shape).
   Early in February the yellow-green mats of foliage and bright yellow flower-balls of this plant become noticeable as scattered clumps in coastal grasslands, a sure sign that spring is on its way. Prostrate, 1/2–1 ft. across; leaves as wide as long, lobed to cleft. Cst. Scr., Grass. Feb.–May.

Gambel Weed or Pacific Sanicle, fig. 86

2. *S. crassicaùlis* (thick-stemmed) [*S. menzièsii*].
   Stem erect, 1–3 ft. tall; leaves 1–3 in. wide and as long; flowers tiny, yellow, the clusters leafy-bracted. Common, shade of woods or brush: many communities. Feb.–May.

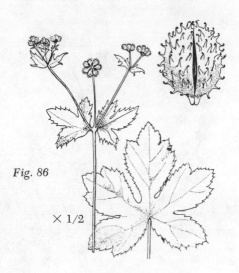

Fig. 86

× 1/2

Coast Sanicle

3. S. *laciniàta* (lacinate or torn, the leaves).

Smaller and more delicate than preceding. Stem 1/2–1 ft. tall; leaves roundish, 1/2–1½ in. wide, 3-lobed, raggedly toothed; flowers yellow. Moist grassy areas or woods or brush near coast. Cl. C. Pine For., Bd. Ev. For., Chap., Grass. Mch. May.

Purple Sanicle, fig. 87

4. S. *bipinnatífida* (2× pinnately cut, the leaves).

Our most abundant Sanicle. Stem 1/2–1 ft. tall; leaves mostly basal, 3–7-lobed, jaggedly toothed; flowers purple, on long leafless branches. Grassy areas: Oak Wood., Chap., Grass. Feb.–May.

Poison Sanicle

5. S. *bipinnàta* (twice pinnate, the leaves).

This species is known to be poisonous to stock, but they seldom feed on it. Root long, swollen, tuber-like;

× 1/2

Fig. 87

stem 1–2 ft. tall; leaves aromatic, the leaflets small; flowers yellow; similar to preceding species in its long, almost leafless branches. Grass or woods: Oak Wood., Grass. Mch.–May.

Turkey Pea or Tuberous Sanicle

6. *S. tuberòsa* (tuberous, the underground stem).

Stem from a pea-like tuber, 1/2–1 ft. tall, simple or branched near ground; leaves with small sharply toothed leaflets; flowers yellow. Dry rocky areas: Oak Wood., Chap. Mch.–May.

Sweet Cicely, fig. 88

Osmorhìza chilénsis (Osmo-rhiza, odor and root, for the aromatic root; *chilensis,* of Chile) [*O. nùda*].

A ferny woodland plant found from Chile to Alaska, called Sweet Cicely because of its anise-flavored roots.

Stem 1½–3 ft. tall; leaves with leaflets 1–2 in. long; flowers tiny, white; fruits long, bristly. Shade: Pon. Pine For., Bd. Ev. For., etc. Apr.–Sept.

Hog Fennel, Wild Parsnip *Lomàtium*

Loma-tium, little border, refers to the wings on the non-bristly, smooth or hairy fruits. Some species with parsnip-like roots were used as food by Indians.

Bladder Parsnip, fig. 89

L. utriculàtum (bladder-like, the leaf bases).

Stem 1/2–1 ft. tall; leaves finely divided, their stalks conspicuously inflated; flowers yellow, each flower-cluster with a circle of green bractlets at base; fruits broadly winged, hairless. Open grassy slopes: Cst. Scr., Oak Wood., etc. Feb.–Apr.

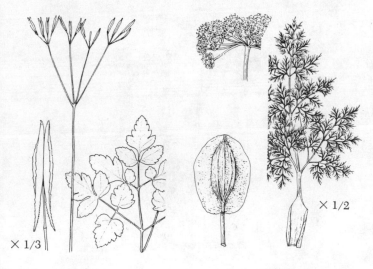

× 1/2

× 1/3

Fig. 88   *Fig.* 89

Lace Parsnip, fig. 90

L. dasycárpum (thick-hairy fruited).

The finely dissected, white-hairy leaves form basal clusters 4–8 in. wide and give a lacy effect to the plants. Flowers on leafless stalks 1–1½ ft. tall, the flower-clusters and their bractlets white-woolly; petals white, fruits densely woolly, thin-winged. Dry rocky soil: mostly Chap. Feb.–May.

Cow Parsnip, fig. 91, pl. 6g

Heraclèum lanàtum (*Heracleum* for Hercules, god of physical strength, because of reputed medicinal value; *lanatum,* woolly, for the foliage).

This coarse stout perennial occurs in colonies on hillsides and becomes weedy in pastures and along fences. A common forage plant, it is reputedly poisonous to stock under some circumstances. Stem 3–9 ft. tall from

× 1/4

Fig. 90

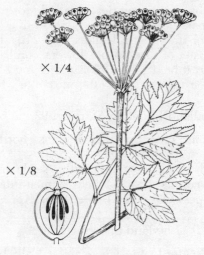

× 1/4

× 1/8

Fig. 91

woody rootstock; leaves huge, with 3 leaflets each 3–6 in. wide; flowers white, in flat-topped clusters 6–10 in. wide. Mostly near coast; many communities. Apr.–July.

There are other less common vernal members of the Parsley Family. Sheep Parsnip *(Lomatium macrocárpum)* is like Lace Parsnip but less hairy, the flowers yellow; woods. Chu-Chu-Pate *(L. califórnicum)* is 2–4 ft. tall, the leaflets 1–3 in. long, hairless, the petals yellow; used medicinally by Indians; woods. Tauschia *(Taùschia hartwègii)* is 1–3 ft. tall, the petals yellow; woods.

PRIMROSE FAMILY *Primulàceae*

Primroses are not to be confused with evening primroses, p. 116. Corolla 4–5-lobed, stamens opposite the lobes.

Shooting Star *Dodecàtheon*

Dodeca-theon, twelve gods, the plants supposedly favored by deities; Shooting Star for the oddly shaped flowers also but less romantically called Mosquito Bills. Perennial; roots fleshy, clustered; leaves in a small flat rosette; flower-stalk single, leafless, 1/2–2 ft. tall, ending in a loose cluster of rose-purple flowers; corolla reflexed upon its short tube, its long lobes projecting backward; stamens erect around style (the mosquito's bill).

Woodland Shooting Star, fig. 92, pl. 5f

D. hendersònii (for L. F. Henderson, northwestern botanist).

Roots with tiny "rice-grain" bulblets which produce new plants; corolla 4- or 5-lobed; stamen-tube purple. Wooded slopes: Oak Wood., etc. Feb.–Apr.

Lowland Shooting Star

D. clevelándii (for Daniel Cleveland, s. Calif. botanist).

Very like preceding but roots lacking bulblets; corolla 5-lobed; stamen-tube purple with 5 yellow spots. Open grassy areas: Cst. Scr., Grass. Jan.–Apr.

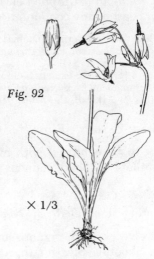

Fig. 92

× 1/3

Star Flower, fig. 93

Trientàlis latifólia (Trientalis, 1/3 ft., for the height; *latifolia,* broad-leaved) [*T. europaéa* var. *latifolia*].

Delicate, the slender stem 4–8 in. tall, at its summit a circle of 3–6 leaves each 1–3 in. long, in the center a loose cluster of 1–4 pink to rose-red, star-like flowers; corolla saucer-shaped, 1/2 in. across, 6-lobed. Shaded moist woods near coast: Redw.-Doug. Fir For., Bd. Ev. For. Mch.–June.

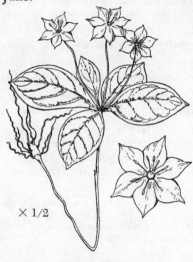

× 1/2

Fig. 93

THRIFT FAMILY *Plumbaginàceae*

Sea Pink, pl. 2c

Armèria marítima var. *califórnica (Armeria,* origin dubious; *maritima,* maritime) [*Státice árctica* var. *californica*].

Leaves linear, erect in a basal tuft 3–6 in. tall; flower-stalk leafless, 1/2–1½ ft. tall, ending in a 1 in.-wide head of pink flowers with papery brown bracts at base. Sturdy plants of ocean bluffs or sandy beaches: Cst. Str., Cst. Scr. Mch.–Aug.

MORNING GLORY FAMILY   *Convolvulàceae*

Morning Glory   *Convólvulus*

Convolvulus, to entwine, refers to the trailing or twining stems. Perennials; flowers showy, funnel- or bowl-shaped, 1½–2 in. long, open only in sun; stamens 5. One introduced weed (*C. arvénsis* – Bindweed) is a pernicious pest in orchards and vineyards.

Beach Morning Glory, pl. 6a

C. soldanélla (small coin, for the round leaves).

Huge pink to purplish flowers amid shining-green, kidney-shaped, leathery leaves trailing in loose sand make this plant memorable. Stem prostrate, 1/2–2 ft. long, deep-rooted; leaves 1–2 in. wide; corolla to 3 in. wide. Ocean beaches: Cst. Str. Apr.–Aug.

Western Morning Glory, fig. 94

C. occidentàlis (western) [*C. lutèolus, C. purpuràtus*].

Attractive but very variable, the long stem trailing on ground or climbing over and entwining in shrubbery; leaves 1–2 in. long, they and flowers scattered along stems; corolla white to cream, pinkish on outside, fading purplish. Brushy or open rocky areas: Cst. Scr., Pon. Pine For., Oak Wood., Chap. Apr.–July.

Hill Morning Glory

C. subacaùlis (somewhat-stemmed) [*C. califórnicus*].

The stem is so short in these plants that their trailing aspect is scarcely manifest. Leaves hairy; corolla as in preceding species. Open rocky hills: Cst. Scr., Oak Wood. Apr.–June.

Phlox Family *Polemoniáceae*

An important family in California's vernal flora. Our
Bay Region species are annuals with 5-lobed calyx, 5-
lobed corolla, 5 stamens on corolla, 3-parted style, and
a capsule with 3 cavities. Genera and species are difficult to tell apart, and the small flowers are no help to
the aspiring botanist attempting a dissection.

Varied-Leaved Collomia, fig. 95

Collòmia heterophýlla (Collomia, glue, for the mucilaginous seeds; *hetero-phylla,* varied-leaved, for the
variable leaves).

Inconspicuous and clammy-glandular, the stem 2–12
in. tall, branching from base; leaves cleft or divided,
to 1+ in. long, very variable; flowers in leafy-bracted
clusters; corolla tubular, rose, 1/2 in. long. Wooded or
brushy areas: many communities. Apr.–July.

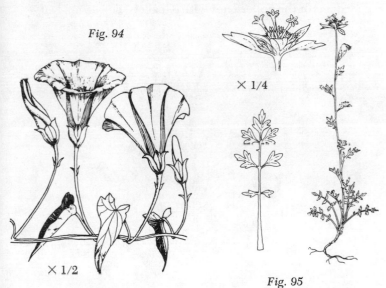

Fig. 94

× 1/4

× 1/2

Fig. 95

Large-flowered Collomia *(Collomia grandiflòra)* is uncommon in woods in our area. Stem 1/2–3 ft. tall; leaves entire; corolla to 1¼ in. long, pale salmon. May–July.

Slender Phlox, fig. 96

Phlóx grácilis (Phlox, flame, for the flower-color; *gracilis,* slender) [*Gília gracilis, Micrósteris gracilis*].

Small, inconspicuous, not like the sweet-scented phloxes of the Sierra. Stem 3–8 in. tall; leaves opposite; flowers scattered, 1/4–1/2 in. long, pink. Open hills: Oak Wood., Grass., etc. Mch.–Apr.

Straggling Gilia   *Allophýllum*

Allo-phyllum, other and leaf, refers to the very variable leaves of these nondescript plants. Two very like species are in our area—*A. gilioìdes* (fig. 97) and *A. divaricàtum* [both formerly known as *Gília gilioides*]. Glandular-hairy, 1/2–2 ft. tall; leaves simple or with several leaflets or the upper ones with 3 leaflets; flowers on leafy

× 1/2

Fig. 96

[130]

branches; corolla blue, 1/2–3/4 in. long, tubular, the lobes spreading. Drying slopes: many communities. Apr.–Sept.

Gilia *Gília*

Gilia was named for F. L. Gil, late eighteenth century Spanish botanist. The species are variable, often difficult to tell apart. Ours have leaves alternate, pinnately lobed or divided, the segments narrow; corolla funnelform, the lobes shorter than tube; stamens attached at throat (top of tube).

Birds' Eyes or Tricolor Gilia, fig. 98

G. tricolor (tricolored, the corolla).

The best known of our gilias, introduced to horticulture along with Globe Gilia in the early 1880's. Stem 4–18 in. tall; foliage somewhat hairy and glandular; flowers 2–5 in small clusters; corolla 1/2–3/4 in. long

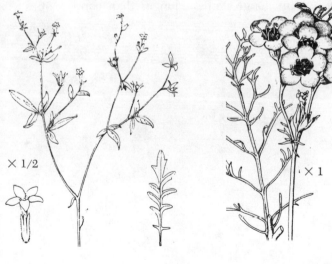

× 1/2

× 1

Fig. 97   Fig. 98

[131]

with yellow tube, 5 deep purple spots (the birds' eyes) or a purple ring in throat, and violet-blue lobes. Sun: Grass., Oak Wood. Feb.–Apr.

California Gilia, fig. 99

G. achilleaefòlia (leaves like *Achillea*, the Common Yarrow) [*G. multicaùlis*, *G. abrotanifòlia*].
Stem slender, 1–3 ft. tall; leaves basal and on stem, smaller upward; flowers 2–25 per cluster; corolla 1/2–3/4 in. long, violet-blue; stamens shorter than corolla lobes. Very variable. Sun or semishade: Bd. Ev. For., Oak Wood., Chap. Mch.–June.

Globe Gilia

G. capitàta (capitate, headed, for the tight flower-cluster).
Like preceding but flowers smaller and 50–100 in dense round heads; corolla pale blue to violet-blue, 1/4–3/8 in. long; stamens longer than corolla lobes.

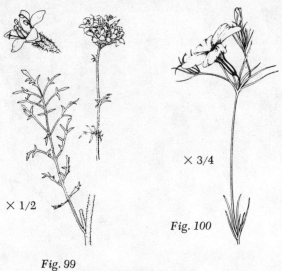

× 3/4

× 1/2

Fig. 100

Fig. 99

[132]

Many subspecies, very variable. Coastal sand-dunes to inland rocky hills: many communities. Apr.–June.

Linanthus *Linánthus*

Linanthus, flax and flower, refers to the sometimes flax-like flowers. The flower-pattern is like that of *Gilia*, but the stem-leaves are opposite, fan-shaped, palmately parted into narrow linear segments. Some species are variable and difficult to distinguish.

Evening Snow, fig. 100

1. *L. dichótomous* (forked in pairs, the branches).
Well-favored by the name Evening Snow, the large, sweetly scented, white flowers open only at dusk. Stem wiry, 2–12 in. tall, often forked; corolla 3/4–1½ in. long; stamens shorter than corolla. Dry slopes: Oak Wood., Chap., Grass. Mch.–May.

Serpentine Linanthus, fig. 101

2. *L. ambíguus* (doubtful, its relationships).

× 1

Fig. 101

Plants small, delicate, in large colonies on soil derived from serpentine rock. Stem 2–8 in. tall; flowers scattered on long stalks; corolla 3/8–3/4 in. long, the lobes pink or blue with a yellowish base, the throat purple. Mostly inland on dry slopes: Oak Wood., Chap., Grass. Apr.–June.

Flax-flowered Linanthus

3. *L. liniflòrus* (flax-flowered) [*L. pharnaceoìdes*].
Like preceding but larger, the stem 1–2 ft. tall, wiry; corolla 1/2–1 in. long, white to pink- or blue-tinged. Dry slopes: Oak Wood., Chap. Apr.–June.

Common Linanthus, fig. 102, pl. 6b

4. *L. androsàceus* (like *Andrósace*, a primrose) [*L. parviflòrus*].
Very common, exceedingly variable, and a very attractive wildflower. Stem 3–14 in. tall; flowers in dense

× 1

Fig. 102

heads; corolla white, cream, yellow, pink, rose, or lavender, with a narrow tube 3/4–1¼ in. long and lobes 1/8–1/2 in. long. Open hills and flats: Cst. Scr., Oak Wood., Chap., Grass. Apr.–July.

Bristly-leaved Linanthus

5. *L. ciliàtus* (ciliate, fringed, the leaves).

Similar to *L. androsaceus* but stiffer, the leaves bristly with coarse hairs, the flowers smaller. Calyx with a conspicuous papery membrane between its lobes; corolla white to rose with yellow throat, the tube 1/2–1 in. long, the lobes 1/8–3/16 in. Dry slopes: Oak Wood., Chap., Grass. Apr.–June.

Bicolored Linanthus

6. *L. bìcolor* (two-colored, the corolla).

Very similar to *L. ciliatus,* but often somewhat smaller, the leaves not quite so bristly-hairy and the calyx lacking a conspicuous papery membrane between its lobes. Open hills: Oak Wood., Chap., Grass. Mch.–May.

PHACELIA FAMILY *Hydrophyllàceae*

Flowers with a deeply 5-parted calyx, 5 stamens attached near corolla-base, an entire, 2-parted or deeply 2-divided style, and a capsule (dry fr.-pod) with 1–2 cavities and few–many seeds.

Fiesta Flower, fig. 103

Pholístoma aurìtum (Pholís-toma, scale and mouth, for the corolla-tube with 5 scales; *auritum,* eared, for the clasping-lobed leaf bases) [*Nemóphila aurìta; Ellísia aurita.*]

Stem 2–6 ft. long, weak and brittle, straggling or climbing by downward-pointed prickles; leaves thin, pinnately lobed; flowers saucer-shaped, to 1 in. wide, bluish-purple. Semishade: Cst. Scr., Oak Wood., Chap., etc. Mch.–June.

Similar in habit and habitat to preceding is White Fiesta Flower *(Pholístoma membranáceum)*. Stem prickleless; flowers white, 1/4 in. wide.

Nemophila *Nemóphila*

Nemophila, grove-loving, refers to woodsy habitat.

Baby Blue-eyes, fig. 104, pl. 6c

N. menzièsii (for Archibald Menzies, one of first botanists on Pacific Coast; in California 1792-1794).

This attractive annual is widespread in California. In 1833 it was first grown in England, where it became a prized garden plant. Stem weak, 1/2–1½ ft. long; leaves opposite, lobed; corolla saucer-shaped, 1/2–1½

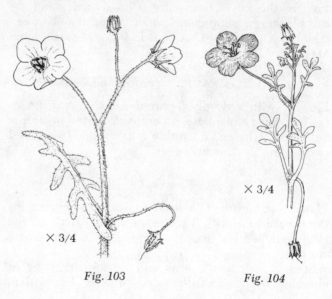

× 3/4

× 3/4

Fig. 103   Fig. 104

in. wide, sky-blue (the baby blue-eyes). Locally common is var. *atomària,* the corolla white with black dots. Grassy or brushy areas, often in plowed fields: Oak Wood., Chap., Grass., Rur. Feb.–Apr.

Small White or Canyon Nemophila

N. heterophýlla (various-leaved, for the variable leaves).

An inconspicuous yet dainty little woodland annual, our most common *Nemophila.* Like preceding in habit, but smaller; stem 1/2–1 or more ft. long; corolla white, 1/4–3/8 in. wide. Shade, hillsides or canyons: Pon. Pine For., Oak Wood., Chap. Feb.–May.

Phacelia *Phacèlia*

Phacelia, cluster, for the crowded flowers arranged in 1-sided spike-like coils. A huge, varied, mostly Californian genus. About 15 species enter the Bay Region, only the more common ones included here. The coarse hairs of some species may cause a dermatitis, but sensitive persons are fortunately few.

California Phacelia, pl. 6d

P. califórnica (of California).

Stout coarsely-hairy perennial 1–2 ft. tall with several stems from base; leaves gray-green, 2–3 in. long, pinnate, the lobes irregular; flowers *ca.* 1/4 in. long, blue-lavender, in coils 1–2 in. long; stamens long. Common on dry rocky soil, mostly coastal: Cst. Scr., Oak Wood., Chap. Mch.–Sept.

Fern Phacelia, fig. 105

P. dístans (standing apart—from its close relatives).

Annual 8–30 in. tall, the stem erect or much-branched; herbage with fine hairs and scattered stiff ones; leaves with fern-like divisions; flowers 1/4–3/8 in. long, whitish to blue, in coils 1–4 in. long; stamens long. Often in colonies—sand-dunes, grassland, or brush: many communities. Mch.–June.

Divaricate Phacelia, fig. 106

P. divaricàta (spreading, the stems).

A beautiful annual with numerous, large, lavender or violet-blue flowers. Stems 1–several from base, 2–12 in. long; leaves oblong to ovate, to 2 in. long, mostly entire; corolla bowl-shaped, 1/2–3/4 in. long, 1 in. wide; stamens shorter than corolla. Rocky soil: Oak Wood., Chap., Grass. Mch.–June.

There are a number of less common phacelias. Rock Phacelia *(P. imbricàta)* is much like Calif. Phacelia but with white flowers; rocky areas inland. Bristly Phacelia *(P. nemoràlis)* is a tall perennial with stinging hairs and whitish flowers; coastal dunes to Mt. Diablo. Branched Phacelia *(P. ramosíssima)* is a tall perennial,

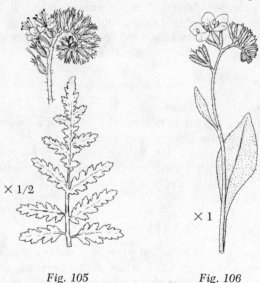

× 1/2

× 1

Fig. 105   Fig. 106

the leaves with large toothed leaflets, the corolla whitish to blue; foothills. Stinging Phacelia *(P. malvaefòlia)* is a coarse annual with bristly hairs, the leaves rounded; shade near coast. Field Phacelia *(P. ciliàta)*, an annual, has the sepals much enlarged in fruit, the corolla blue; clay soil inland, often abundant in fallow fields. Brewer's Phacelia *(P. brèweri)*, is a slender annual with softly hairy foliage and blue corolla, Mt. Diablo and Mt. Hamilton Range.

Mist Maiden, fig. 107

Romanzóffia suksdórfii (genus for Count Romanzoff, patron of Chamisso, German botanist who found this in 1816; species for Wm. N. Suksdorf, Washington botanist, 1850-1932) [*R. sitchénsis; R. califórnica*].

Mist Maiden is a low fragile plant of moist mossy ledges. Stem 4–10 in. tall, from hairy, white, underground tubers; leaves mostly basal, round, lobed, hairless; flowers on slender stalks, white, 1/4–3/8 in. long. Shade of coastal forests: Redw.-Doug. Fir For., Bd. Ev. For. Mch.–May.

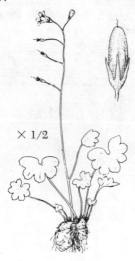

× 1/2

Fig. 107

Borage Family   *Boraginàceae*

Borages, like phacelias, are rough or bristly with coarse hairs and with flowers in one-sided, often spike-like coils; they differ in having a deeply 4-lobed ovary which matures into 1–4 hard nutlets (best seen on lowest and oldest flowers of a coil).

Hounds Tongue, fig. 108

Cynoglóssum gránde (Cyno-glossum, dog and tongue, for the shape and texture of leaves; *grande,* large).

Our only borage with a claim to stateliness. Stem 1–3 ft. tall from a woody root; leaves lance-shaped, large, long-stalked, hairy beneath; flowers in small loose coils, blue (pink in bud), with a ring of white crests in throat (like forget-me-nots). Moist woods: Pon. Pine For., Bd. Ev. For., Oak Wood. Feb.–May.

Apt to be considered a native wildflower is the European Forget-me-not *(Myosòtis sylvática)* which has escaped from gardens and established itself in our coastal forests.

× 1/8

Fig. 108

Fiddleneck *Amsínckia*

Fiddlenecks are coarse bristly-hairy annuals with small orange flowers in long coils, very abundant in California's flora, although they are more apt to be considered weeds than native wildflowers. Named for Wm. Amsinck, Hamburg botanical patron.

Common Fiddleneck, fig. 109

A. intermèdia (intermediate—in distinguishing characteristics) [*A. douglasiàna* of some authors].

Stem erect, often widely branching, to 2½ ft. tall; flowers *ca.* 1/4 in. wide, yellow-orange in coiled spikes. Fields, ditches, roadsides, etc., often weedy on disturbed soils: many communities. Mch.–June.

Coast Fiddleneck

A. spectábilis (spectacular, showy, the flowers) [*A. intermèdia* var. *spectabilis*].

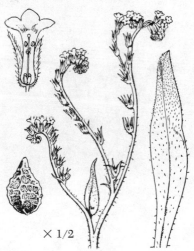

× 1/2

Fig. 109

[141]

For a Fiddleneck the yellow-orange flowers are very showy, but they scarcely redeem the coarseness of the rest of the plant. Stems sprawling 1–2 ft., flowers 3/8–1/2 in. wide, in long coiled spikes. Sand: Cst. Str., Cst. Salt Marsh, Cst. Scr. Mch.–July.

Valley Fiddleneck (*A. eastwoòdiae*, pl. 7a) has deep orange flowers as large as those of Coast Fiddleneck; low fields, e. Contra Costa and Alameda Cos.

White Forget-me-not *Cryptántha*

These are small, wiry, coarsely or bristly hairy, inconspicuous annuals of dry areas. *Cryp-tantha*, hidden and flower, refers to the small flowers which have white corollas of Forget-me-not shape. The most common species in our area are: *C. fláccida* (fig. 110), nutlets 1 per flower, on rocky slopes in open or in chaparral, Apr.–June; *C. torreyàna*, nutlets 4, otherwise similar, grasslands or valley flats, May–June.

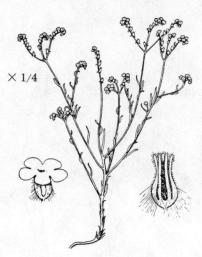

× 1/4

Fig. 110

Popcorn Flower *Plagiobóthrys*

Slender annuals with white flowers of the Forget-Me-Not type which, in their abundance and whiteness, simulate popped corn. Much like *Cryptantha* (above), but foliage more softly hairy and nutlets very different. The various species are hard to tell apart, and only representative ones are given below. *Plagio-bothrys*, on-the-side and pit, refers to nutlet attachment.

Valley Popcorn Flower, fig. 111

P. stipitàtus (stalked, the nutlets) [*Allocàrya stipitata*].
Stems many, prostrate, spreading 1–1½ ft., flowers 1/8–1/4 in. wide, with a yellow center which fades white. Common, low wet fields, e. Contra Costa and Alameda Cos.: Grass. Mch.–May.

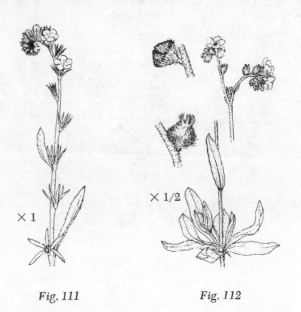

Fig. 111   Fig. 112

Common Popcorn Flower or
Foothill Snowdrops, fig. 112

P. nothofúlvus (falsely fulvus, i.e., not the related *P. fulvus*).

This well-known Popcorn Flower is also called Foothill Snowdrops because of the myriad of small, fragrant, white flowers it produces on grassy hillsides in early spring. Stem erect, branching above, 1/2–2 ft. tall; leaves mostly in a basal rosette, containing a purple dye. Common, fields and hillsides: Cst. Scr., Oak Wood., Grass. Feb.–June.

MINT FAMILY *Labiàtae*

Mints are told by the aromatic minty odor of the foliage, square stems with opposite leaves, and flowers with a 2-lipped corolla (3 lobes above, 2 below), 2 or 4 stamens, and a deeply 4-lobed ovary.

× 2/3

Fig. 113

Skull Cap, fig. 113

Scutellària tuberòsa (*Scutella-ria*, little dish, because of the bulge at calyx-base, hence also Skull Cap; *tuberosa*, the underground stems tuberous).

Perennial with small white tubers giving rise to clustered leafy stems 2–8 in. tall; corolla blue, *ca.* 3/4 in. long. In colonies, moist soil of woods or brush: Pon. Pine For., Oak Wood., Chap. Mch.–May.

Sage *Sálvia*

Calyx 2-lipped, the teeth spiny; corolla with the lower lip often much larger than upper; one pair of stamens sterile or aborted. A very diverse group. *Salvia* means to save (some of the species are medicinal).

Chia, fig. 114

S. *columbàriae* (dove-cote, for the appearance of the densely clustered flowers).

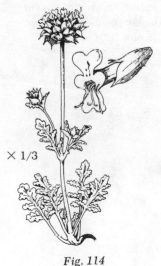

× 1/3

Fig. 114

Chia, the Indian name of this famous plant, means strong or strengthening, as the tiny mucilaginous seeds are very nourishing and are also valued medicinally. From aboriginal times they were a dietary staple of southwestern Indians and later became important to Spanish-Californians. They were eaten raw or roasted or were ground for use in *pinole.* Annual with erect stem 1/2–1½ ft. tall; leaves gray-green, thick, rough, mostly basal; flowers in 1–2 dense red- or purplish-bracted whorls (circles) terminating stem; corolla vivid blue. Dry hills: Cst. Scr., Oak Wood., Chap., Grass. Mch.–July.

Another mint, Self Heal *(Prunélla vulgàris)* occurs in our area both as a weed, which in Europe has had long use as a folk medicine (subsp. *vulgàris*), and as a native (subsp. *lanceolàta*). The latter is a creeping perennial 4–10 in. tall with soft-hairy leaves and flowers in a single, dense, purplish spike at stem-tip; corolla violet. Mostly ocean bluffs. Apr.–Dec.

Hedge Nettle, fig. 115

Stàchys rígida subsp. *quercetòrum (Stachys,* ear of corn, for the spike-like flower-clusters; *rigida,* rigid, the calyx; *quercetorum,* of oak groves).

× 1

Fig. 115

Hedge Nettle isn't a nettle, but perhaps the folk call it so because it grows along roadsides and its calyx is prickly. Perennial, the stem leafy, 1–2 ft. tall; leaves 1–3 in. long; flowers in 3–8 circles on stem; corolla pink mottled with rose. Woods or open areas: Cst. Scr., Bd. Ev. For., Oak Wood. Mch.–July.

In moist areas of the Santa Cruz Mts. is a very similar Hedge Nettle, S. *bullàta*. Both S. *rigida* and S. *bullata* have a ring of hairs inside the corolla tube; in S. *rigida* it shows on the outside as a constriction, while in S. *bullata* it does not.

Yerba Buena, fig. 116

Saturèja douglásii (Satureja, Arabic name for mints; *douglasii,* for David Douglas, California's most famous early plant collector) [*Micromèria chamissònis*].

Yerba Buena is indeed a "good herb," for the dried leaves make not only a very tasty tea but one which gives relief from fever and digestive disorders. A pretty trailing plant with glossy evergreen leaves, the small

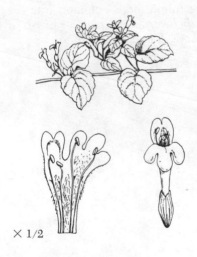

× 1/2

Fig. 116

white flowers on the stem 1 per leaf. In woods or brush mostly near the coast: Redw.-Doug. Fir For., Bd. Ev. For., Chap. May–Aug.

Nightshade Family *Solanàceae*

This family is notable for food plants (Pòtato, Tomato) and poisonous or medicinal plants (Belladonna or Deadly Nightshade, Jimson Weed, Tobacco). It has many weedy species in our area, but only one native which is a spring-blooming herb.

Purple Nightshade, fig. 117

Solànum xántii var. *intermèdium (Solanum,* the origin dubious; *xantii,* for L. J. Xantus, early Pacific Coast collector; *intermedium,* intermediate—to species).

Stems herbaceous, many from a woody root, 1–2 ft. tall, with leaves 1–3 in. long; flowers violet-blue, saucer-shaped, 1/2–1 in. wide, with 5 erect yellow stamens. Very like the much more common but shrubby Blue Witch *(S. umbellíferum).* Woods or brush on dry rocky soil. Oak Wood., Chap. Mch.–June.

× 3/4

Fig. 117

Figwort Family *Scrophulariàceae*

The Figwort Family is known in California for its pleni-
tude of colorful and showy spring wildflowers and for
such garden favorites as penstemons, monkey flowers,
snapdragons, foxgloves, etc. Stem round (or square);
leaves alternate or opposite; corolla 2-lipped (2 lobes
above, 3 below); stamens 2, 4, or 5; ovary unlobed, becoming a 2-cavitied, many-seeded capsule.

Chinese Houses, Blue-eyed Mary *Collínsia*

Collinsia commemorates Z. Collins, early American botanist. Chinese Houses describe the pagoda-like flower-
whorls of some species. Others with scattered blue
flowers have the quaint name of Blue-eyed Mary. Annuals; leaves opposite; middle of lower lip of corolla
boat-shaped, enclosing style and 4 stamens.

Chinese Houses, pl. 6f

C. heterophýlla (variable-leaved) [*C. bicolor*].
   This, our most frequent *Collinsia,* has been a favorite
in English gardens for over 100 years. Stem 1/2–1½ ft.
tall; leaves 1–2 in. long; flowers in 1–5 whorls on stem;
corolla whitish to red-purple, 1/2–7/8 in. long; upper
pair of stamens with short, upturned, basal horns. Open
woods or grassy slopes: Oak Wood., Chap., Grass. Apr.–
June.

Two other large-flowered species of Chinese Houses, both
lacking basal horns on the stamens, are: *C. tinctòria,* leaves
staining brown, flowers white to yellowish, mainly from Napa
and Sonoma Cos. to Mt. Diablo, May–Aug.; and *C. bartsiae-
folia,* corolla white tinged with purple, the upper lip short, in
sandy coastal soil from San Francisco s., Apr.–June.

Blue-eyed Mary, fig. 118

C. sparsiflòra (few-flowered).

This species includes both large- and small-flowered varieties, the corolla from 1/4 in. long (var. *solitaria*, figured) to 3/4 in. (var. *arvénsis*). Stem slender, 4–12 in. tall; leaves about 1 in. long; flowers buff-yellow to blue, scattered. Open slopes: Oak Wood., Grass., etc. Mch.–May.

California Bee Plant, fig. 119

Scrophulària califórnica (Scrophularia, once thought a remedy for scrofula; *calif, californica,* of California).

Bee Plant is a rank perennial 3–6 ft. tall, the foliage attracting more attention than the many, small, maroon flowers which the bees, however, do not neglect. Leaves opposite, 2–4 in. long, toothed. Moist areas in brush or woods: many communities. Feb.–July.

Foothill Penstemon, pl. 7c

Pénstemon heterophýllus (Penstemon, with 5 stamens; *heterophyllus,* variable-leaved). [*Pentstèmon*].

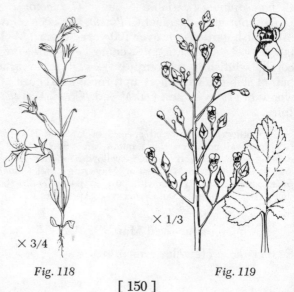

× 3/4

× 1/3

Fig. 118　　　　　　　　*Fig. 119*

This *Penstemon* has been grown in European gardens since explorer David Douglas collected seeds of it over 100 years ago. It has many reddish stems 1–2 ft. tall from a woody base, narrow opposite leaves, and a profusion of large flowers 1–1½ in. long, the corolla violet with blue lobes, the buds yellowish. Dry hillsides: Oak Wood., Chap. May–June.

Common Monkey Flower, pl. 7d

Mímulus guttàtus (Mimulus, buffoon, the flowers with monkey faces; *guttatus,* speckled, the flowers).

Found throughout California in water seepages, along streams, etc., extremely variable in size and form. Its juicy leaves can be eaten as a salad-green. Stem stout, 1–2 ft. tall; leaves opposite, irregularly toothed; flowers in a raceme; corolla yellow, 3/4–1½ in. long, usually speckled with red or brown. Wet places: many communities. Jan.–Oct.

Paint Brush   *Castillèja*

Castilleja was named for a Spanish botanist, D. Castillejo. The species of this large, well-known and colorful genus hybridize readily and are often hard to tell apart. The plants are root-parasites on other kinds of plants. The inconspicuous flowers are in long spikes, each flower with a usually 3–5-lobed, fan-like bract (leaf) beneath it. The bracts give the plume-like form and most of the gaudy color to the spikes (the paint brushes). Perennials; stems 1/2–2 ft. tall, 1–several from a woody base; leaves alternate, simple or 1–4-lobed; calyx tubular, 2-lipped; upper corolla-lip long, narrow, enclosing style and stamens, the lower lip 3-lobed, very short.

Indian Paint Brush, pl. 7b

1. *C. affìnis* (related—to other species) [*C. douglásii;*

C. parviflòra var. *douglasii;* confused with *C. francis-càna* by some authors].

Leaves usually lobed, thin, rough-hairy; bracts and calyces[3] scarlet; corolla green with red margins, its upper lip to 1 in. long, its lower lip short, hidden within calyx. Open hills, woods or brush, not coastal: many communities. Mch.–Aug.

Seaside Paint Brush, fig. 120

2. *C. wìghtii* (for W. F. Wight of U.S. Dept. of Agri.) [*C. latifòlia* var. *wightii; C. latifolia* of some authors].

Glandular-hairy; leaves entire or with 1–3 often short lobes, thick; bracts and calyces yellow or apricot to dull scarlet; corolla yellow-green, its lower lip hidden within calyx. Coastal hills and seashore: Cst. Str., Cst. Scr., Bd. Ev. For. Mch.–July.

× 1/2

Fig. 120

---

[3] plural of calyx

Woolly Paint Brush

3. *C. foliolòsa* (with many leaves).
White-woolly; leaves often 3-lobed, with clusters of
smaller leaves crowded in at base of each lower leaf;
bracts and calyces dull scarlet; corolla yellow-green,
its lower lip hidden in calyx. Dry brushy slopes: Chap.
Mch.–Aug.

Franciscan Paint Brush, pl. 7f

4. *C. franciscàna* (of San Francisco) [confused by some
authors with *C. affinis*, first species above].
Grayish green, to 2 ft. tall; leaves mostly unlobed;
bracts and calyces bright scarlet; corolla yellow-green,
to 1¾ in. long, the lower lip visible above the slit in
calyx. Woods, brush, or open coastal hills: Cst. Scr.,
Chap. Mch.–Sept.

Owl's Clover   *Orthocárpus*

Owl's clovers are abundant and colorful in California's
vernal flora. There is no obvious relation with owls or
Clover, but *Orthocarpus* means straight and fruit in
reference to the erect capsules. Like paint brushes
(above) in their long flower-plumes, each flower with
a fan-like, often brightly colored bract (leaf) beneath
it. Annuals; leaves alternate, usually deeply lobed;
corolla with a short stubby upper lip and a large lower
lip with 3 pouches.

Dwarf Owl's Clover

1. *O. pusíllus* (very small).
Inconspicuous, 2–10 in. tall, revealed by its purplish
foliage when it grows in dense colonies in grass. Flowers
red-purple, very small, scattered. Open flats and slopes:
Oak Wood., Grass. Mch.–May.

[153]

2. *O. floribúndus* (blooming profusely).

A rare plant of coastal grasslands known only from Pt. Reyes in Marin Co. to San Mateo Co. Stem 4–12 in. tall, branched; flowers in short dense spikes; corolla white to cream, 1/2 in. long; stamens longer than upper lip. Cst. Scr. Mch.–May.

Butter-and-eggs or Johnny Tuck, fig. 121, pl. 7e

3. *O. eriánthus* (woolly flowered, the corolla ± hairy).

It is easy to see how this bright yellow-flowered plant came to be kown as Butter-and-Eggs, but the Johnny Tuck remains a mystery. Stem 4–12 in. tall, the foliage often purplish; corolla 1/2–1 in. long, the upper lip small, purple, the 3 pouches of the lower lip very inflated, yellow. Abundant in fields or open woods: Oak Wood., Grass. Mch.–Apr. Coastal plants have flowers white or pink with upper lip purple (var. *ròseus*). Cst. Scr. Apr.–May.

× 3/4

Fig. 121

[154]

4. *O. faucibarbàtus* (throat hairy, the corolla throat).
Stem 6–20 in. tall; foliage green, lacking hairs
(smooth); flowers 3/4 in. long, lemon-yellow, like
those of *O. erianthus* but upper lip not purple. Low
fields n. of S.F. Bay: Oak Wood., Grass. Along coast
both n. and s. of the Bay are white-flowered plants
fading pink (var. *álbidus*): Cst. Scr. Apr.–June.

Cream Sacs

5. *O. lithospermoìdes* (like *Lithospérmum*, a Borage).
Stem 8–14 in. tall, mostly unbranched; foliage green,
hairy; flowers 1–1¼ in. long, cream, shaped much as
in *O. faucibarbatus* above. Open slopes: Oak Wood.,
Chap., Grass. Apr.–June.

Valley Tassels

6. *O. attenuàtus* (narrowed to a point, the leaves).

× 1

Fig. 122

Stem 4–16 in. tall, usually unbranched; foliage green, short-hairy; floral bracts usually white- or purplish-tipped; flowers 1/2–3/4 in. long; corolla white to purplish, the lower lip with 3 teeth about as long as the upper lip and 3 shallow purple-dotted pouches. Abundant, valleys or open hills: Pon. Pine For., Oak Wood., Grass., etc. Apr.–May.

Owl's Clover, pl. 8c

7. *O. densiflòrus* (densely flowered, for the flower-spike).

This and the next colorful species are thought of by most people as the true owl's clovers. Stem 4–16 in. tall, often branched; foliage green, finely hairy; bracts tipped with rose-purple; flowers 3/4 in. long, with rose-purple calyx and corolla, the upper lip of corolla slightly hairy, straight, the knob-like stigma protruding from it, the lower lip often yellowish with purple spots, its teeth almost as long as upper lip. Common, valleys or open hills: Cst. Scr., Oak Wood., Grass. Mch.–May.

Purple Owl's Clover or Escobita, pl. 7g

8. *O. purpuráscens* (purplish, the flower-spike).

Spanish-Californians called this most beautiful of all owl's clovers *Escobita*, little broom, because of the densely clumped flower-spikes. Under a hand-lens the flowers are exquisite creations, complicated beyond belief. They are very similar to those of *O. densiflorus* but even more elaborate, the upper lip being heavily bearded and hooked at the tip. Common, valleys or open hills: Cst. Scr., Oak Wood., Grass. Mch.–May.

Indian Warrior, fig. 123

Pediculàris densiflòra (Pedicularis, from louse, due to an old superstition that sheep eating it became lousy; *densiflora,* densely flowered, the raceme).

[156]

The beautiful, fern-like, red-purplish leaves of this woodland plant are finely cut, and the deep red flowers are in long bracted racemes. Stem 8–20 in. tall; leaves 8–10 in. long; corolla *ca*. 1 in. long, the wide upper lip arched, the lower lip short. Woods and brush: Pon. Pine For., Oak Wood., Chap. Jan.–July.

Bellardia trixago, with pretty white or white and pink flowers, is a European introduction found in old fields. Annual, 6–18 in. tall; leaves toothed, opposite, lance-shaped. Apr.–May.

PLANTAIN FAMILY *Plantaginàceae*

Dwarf Plantain, fig. 124

Plantàgo erécta (Plantago, plantain; *erecta*, erect, the stems) [*P. hookeriàna* var. *califórnica*].

This small drab annual occurs in great numbers in open grassland. Look with a hand-lens to find beauty of form and texture in the small, 4-parted, silvery-papery flowers. Leaves long, narrow, basal; flower-

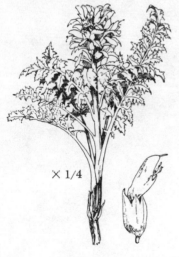

× 1/4

Fig. 123

× 1

Fig. 124

stalks 2–10 in. tall, each ending in a short crowded flower-spike. Hills and valleys: Cst. Scr., Oak Wood., Chap., Grass. Feb.–June.

VALERIAN FAMILY   *Valerianàceae*

Plectritis   *Plectrìtis*

These slender annuals, common enough on openly wooded slopes, lack a common name. *Plectritis* is probably from cock's spur, each white to pink corolla having a basal spur. Our three species are much alike: *P. cilìòsa* (fig. 125), *P. congésta*, and *P. macrócera*. Biologically they are interesting in that each species produces plants with both narrow- and broad-winged fruits. Oak Wood., Grass., etc. Apr.–May.

CUCUMBER FAMILY   *Cucurbitàceae*

Manroot or Wild Cucumber, fig. 126

Màrah fabàceus (*Marah*, bitterness; *fabaceus*, bean-like, the seeds) [*Echinocýstis fabàcea*].

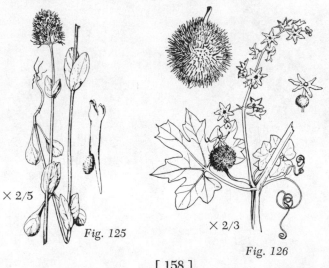

× 2/5

Fig. 125

× 2/3

Fig. 126

This vine climbs to 20 or 30 ft. by means of tendrils. Amazingly the slender stems come from a root which may weigh over 50 pounds and be as large as and often shaped like a man's body (Manroot). The bitter poisonous juice of the roots was used by Indians medicinally and to stupify fish. The hard round seeds, also somewhat toxic if ingested, have been used for marbles, jackstones, beads, etc. Leaves ivy-like, 2–4 in. wide; flowers in small racemes, yellowish green, saucer-shaped, 1/2 in. wide; fruit densely spiny, *ca.* 2 in. long. Sand-dunes, woods or brush: Cst. Str., Bd. Ev. For., Oak Wood., Chap. Mch.–May.

Another very similar Wild Cucumber (*M. oregànus*) is fairly common near the coast. Flowers bowl-shaped; fruits not densely spiny, the spines scattered, weak.

Sunflower Family *Compósitae*

This, the largest and most highly developed family of flowering plants, has small and numerous flowers in dense heads which look like single flowers. Around the base of each head are 1 or more rows of green bracts which are collectively known as an *involucre*. Typically the head has many tubular *disk*-flowers encircled by a row of strap-shaped *ray*-flowers, or the head may have all tubular or all strap-shaped flowers. The family has many ornamentals (daisies, marigolds, dahlias, chrysanthemums, etc.), many weeds (ragweeds, sow thistles, etc.), and some food plants (Sunflower "seeds", Lettuce, Endive, etc.). Ovary beneath corolla (inferior); calyx absent or present as a ring of hairs, bristles, or scales (*pappus*, best seen in mature heads); stamens 5, the anthers united in a tube around the 2-parted style; fruit dry, containing (and looking like) a single seed, usually many per head.

Microseris *Micróseris*

These nondescript plants may not look like Lettuce but they are related, hence *Micro-seris*, which means small and lettuce-like. They are annuals with a basal clump of short pinnate leaves and tall leafless flower-stalks, each stalk ending in a nodding, closed, inconspicuous head of strap-shaped flowers. After flowering these heads become erect and wide-open to expose the cylindrical fruits each topped by a pappus of 5 papery scales ending in bristles. Our two most frequent species are: Silver Puffs *(M. douglàsii,* fig. 127), its silvery pappus-scales narrowed gradually into bristles; and Narrow-leaved Microseris *(M. linearifòlia)* [*Uropáppus l.*], its straw-color pappus-scales notched below the bristles. Both are species of open grassland: Cst. Scr., Oak Wood., Grass. Mch.–May.

Western Dandelion   *Agòseris*

Ago-seris means goat and lettuce-like. Whatever the connection with goats, the plants are related to Lettuce

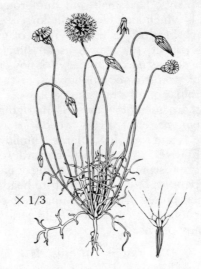

× 1/3

Fig. 127

[160]

and even more closely to European Dandelion, a well-known garden weed. Annuals or perennials with toothed, elongate, basal leaves and long flower-stalks each ending in a large head of yellow strap-shaped flowers; fruits ribbed, the slender beaks each ending in a parachute-like tuft of white hairs. Several species occur in our area, among them: California Dandelion (*A. grandiflòra*) [*A. plebèia*], perennial, and Mountain Dandelion (*A. heterophýlla*, fig. 128), annual, both of grassy slopes or valley-flats, Jan.–Sept., and Seaside Dandelion (*A. apargioìdes*), perennial, coastal bluffs or sand-dunes, Mch.–Nov.

Woolly Malacothrix, fig. 129

Malacóthrix floccífera (*Malaco-thrix*, soft and hair, because of the woolly hairs; *flocc-ifera*, full of flocks of wool, the leaves) [*M. obtùsa*].

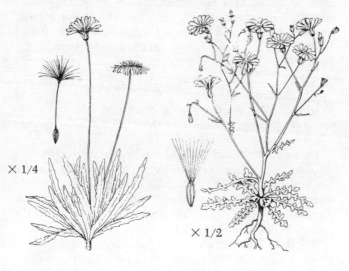

× 1/4

× 1/2

Fig. 128   *Fig. 129*

A pretty little annual with leaves in a flat basal rosette and branching stems 4–16 in. tall. Leaves narrow, pinnately toothed, their margins with scattered tufts of wool; heads numerous, of strap-shaped white flowers tinged with pink. Dry rocky hillsides: Oak Wood., Chap., mostly in interior. Apr.–Aug.

Gum Weed *Grindèlia*

Gum weeds are coarse summer-blooming perennials whose large yellow flower-heads brighten dry hillsides. The herbage and especially the several rows of bracts (involucre) below each flower-head have a white-gummy resinous exudate which has made the plants useful medicinally in such disorders as asthma and bronchitis. The genus was named for H. Grindel, Russian botanist. Two species start to bloom in late spring: *G. campòrum*, the most common species, in which the foliage lacks hairs, is found on road-banks, in dry fields, or in low alkaline areas, May–Sept., and *G. hirsùtula*, the foliage somewhat hairy and the stems often reddish, is found on dry open or brushy hills from the coast inland, Apr.–July.

Seaside Daisy, pl. 8a

Erìgeron gláucus (*Eri-geron*, early and old man—old man of spring; *glaucus*, with a bloom, the leaves whitish).

These colorful daisies add much beauty to seacoast rock-gardens. They occur in nature only on sand-dunes, ocean bluffs, or windswept hills near the coast in California and Oregon, yet they were grown in English gardens and described and named there in 1815, the source of seed unknown! Perennial with sturdy stems 1/2–1 ft. tall; leaves numerous, somewhat viscid; heads 1¼–1½ in. wide, with many lilac to violet ray-flowers around a center of yellow disk-flowers. Cst. Str., Cst. Scr. Mch.–Aug.

Wyethia was named for Capt. Nathaniel J. Wyeth who discovered these sunflower-like plants in 1834. Only a little imagination is required to see the large, erect, basal leaves as mules' ears at attention. The large "seeds" (fruits) were parched, ground, and made into *pinole* by California Indians, while the young leaves of some species were eaten raw as salad and the fermented roots were used both as food and medicine. Perennials with stout woody roots, tufts of long basal leaves, and stems 1–2 ft. tall with smaller alternate leaves; flower-heads 2–4 in. wide, both ray- and disk-flowers yellow.

Narrow-leaved Mule Ears, fig. 130

W. angustifòlia (narrow-leaved).

Foliage green; bracts of flower-heads 1/2–1 in. long, oblongish, fringed with white hairs. Common on open hills: Oak Wood., Chap., Grass. Mch.–June.

× 1/6

Fig. 130

Gray Mule Ears, pl. 8b

W. helenioìdes (like *Helènium,* another sunflower).

Foliage gray with dense soft hairs; bracts of flower-heads 1–3 in. long, ovate. Common on open hills: Pon. Pine For., Oak Wood., Grass. Mch.–June.

Much like *W. helenioides* is *W. glàbra,* but with foliage green, sticky, balsam-scented. Edge of forest or brush in partial shade, uncommon: Doug. Fir For., Bd. Ev. For., Chap. Mch.–June.

California Helianthella, pl. 8d

Helianthélla califórnica (*Helianth-ella,* little sunflower; *californica,* of California) [*H. castànea*].

Much like true Sunflower (*Heliánthus*) but even more like Mule Ears (above). Stem leaves mostly opposite; flower-heads 1½–2 in. wide, yellow. Woods or open, mostly inner Coast Ranges: Oak Wood., Grass. May–June.

Coreopsis *Coreópsis*

Core-opsis, bug and appearance, gained its name from the quaint idea that the "seeds" (fruits) look like bugs, understandable when one sees ripe fruits. Many people know the garden Coreopsis, but most are unaware that California has some very pretty native species. Slightly succulent annuals 4–16 in. tall; leaves usually pinnate or bipinnate; bracts (involucre) of the flower-head in 2 rows—inner row with bracts closely erect around flowers, outer row with bracts narrow, spreading; both disk- and ray-flowers golden-yellow. Two species occur on open rocky slopes in the interior of the Mt. Hamilton Range, Mch.–May, both with basal leaves and flower-heads 3/4–1 in. wide: *C. stillmánii* (fig. 131), its leaves flatish and pinnate or bipinnate, and *C. douglásii,* its leaves linear, fleshy, and entire or with 1–2 linear lobes. In Corral Hollow *C. calliopsídea* is found, its leaves both basal and on stem, and its flower-heads up to 3 in. wide.

Springtime Tarweed, fig. 132

Hemizònia multicaùlis subsp. *vernàlis* (*Hemi-zonia,* half and zone, each bract of involucre half enclosing the fruit of a ray-flower; *multi-caulis,* many-stemmed; *vernalis,* of spring) [*H. luzulaefòlia* var. *citrìna*].

The tarweeds, which include both this genus (*Hemizonia*) and the next *(Madia),* bloom in summer or autumn and are mostly sticky, smelly, unattractive plants. But this one is an exception; its plants open their showy, clear yellow flower-heads while there is still verdure in the grasslands, and their grass-like leaves are silvery silky. Slender annual 4–20 in. tall, its upper half somewhat sticky; flower-heads 8–20, 1–1½ in. wide. Open grassy areas away from seacoast, Sonoma and Marin Cos.: Oak Wood., Grass. Apr.–July.

On ocean bluffs in Sonoma and Marin Cos. Seaside Tar-weed (*H. multicaùlis* subsp. *multicaùlis*) blooms later (May–July), its leaves neither grass-like nor silvery as in subsp. *vernalis* above.

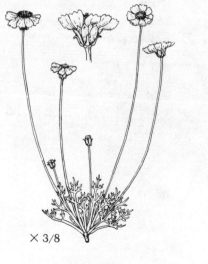

× 3/8

Fig. 131

× 1/4

Fig. 132

[165]

Madia or Tarweed *Màdia*

Madia comes from the Chilean name for these plants. Like the preceding genus, most of these tarweeds also bloom in summer or fall and are sticky, smelly, and even repulsive. Happily, however, those in our spring flora are attractive plants. The "seeds" (fruits) of these tarweeds are nutritious and were used by Californian Indians in preparing *pinole*. The bracts around the heads each completely enfold a ray-flower. Leaves opposite on lower part of stem, alternate near top, linear, the lower ones 3–5 in. long; both ray- and disk-flowers yellow.

Woodland Madia

M. madioìdes (like *Madia*).

Perennial 1–2½ ft. tall, hairy below and somewhat glandular above; flower-heads few, not showy, 1/2–3/4 in. wide. Moist banks in forests or woods: Redw. Doug. Fir For., Bd. Ev. For. Apr.–Sept.

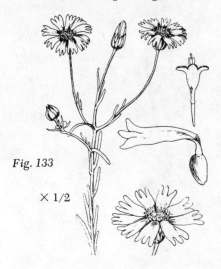

Fig. 133

× 1/2

Springtime Madia, fig. 133

M. élegans subsp. *vernàlis (elegans,* elegant; *vernalis,* belonging to spring).

Springtime Madia blooms in spring in about the same areas occupied by Common Madia (*M. elegans* subsp. *elegans*) in summer and fall. Annual 3/4–2 ft. tall, rather rough-hairy and sticky; flower-heads bright yellow and showy, 1 1½ in. wide. Grassy or wooded slopes: Oak Wood., Chap., Grass. Apr.–July.

A beautiful but very localized Madia is *M. nutans,* found only among volcanic rocks in mountains of Napa and Sonoma Cos. The many flower-heads hang down in bud. Oak wood., Chap. Apr.–May.

Layia   *Làyia*

Layia, named for G. T. Lay, a botanist who visited California in 1827, is akin to tarweeds (*Hemizonia* and *Madia* above), but the plants are vernal annuals with little or no stickiness and with usually showy flower-heads. Leaves alternate; flower-heads all yellow-flowered or the rays tipped with white; bracts of involucre as in *Madia,* each completely enfolding the fruit of a ray-flower. In our species the anthers of the disk-flowers are black.

Tidy Tips, pl. 8e

L. platyglóssa (flat tongue, for the ray-flowers).

These handsome plants owe their beauty to the large yellow flower-heads whose ray-flowers are tipped with creamy white (the tidy tips). Annual 4–16 in. tall; leaves rough-hairy, somewhat glandular; flower-heads to 1½ in. wide. Common, coastal dunes to inland valleys: Cst. Scr., Grass. Mch.–Sept.

Smooth Layia, fig. 134

L. chrysanthemoìdes (like *Chrysánthemum*) [*L. calli-glóssa*].

Another beautiful species with flower-heads white-tipped and so like those of Tidy Tips that it is not easy to tell them apart at first. But Smooth Layia has non-hairy, nonglandular leaf-surfaces, although the leaf-margins are rough-hairy. Locally abundant in low fields: Grass. Apr.–June.

Woodland Layia

L. gaillardioìdes (similar to *Gaillàrdia*).

Slender or occas. coarse annual 1/2–2 ft. tall with rough-hairy herbage, dark spots on the stem, and golden to pale yellow flower-heads 3/4–1¼ in. wide. Grassy, wooded, or brushy areas: Oak Wood., Chap., Grass. Apr.–July.

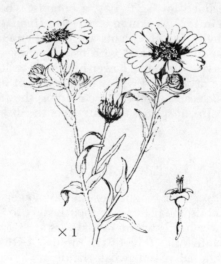

× 1

Fig. 134

Blow Wives, pl. 8f

Achyrachaèna móllis (*Achyr-achaena*, chaff and achene, for the chaffy fruits; *mollis*, soft-hairy, the foliage).

These odd plants are almost unnoticeable when in flower, for the reddish-tipped ray- and disk-flowers scarcely show above the erect green bracts of the heads. But in fruit the heads open into silvery puffs 1½ in. wide which await only sudden motion to disperse the fruits each crowned with a spreading cluster of chaffy pappus scales. Open areas: Oak Wood., Chap. Mch.–May.

Gold Fields *Baèria*

In spring the golden-yellow flower-heads produced by multitudes of these small plants turn slopes and valleys into fields of gold, and so arose the common name. The genus was named by Russian botanists for a Russian zoologist, K. E. Baer, the seeds probably having been sent to Russia from the Russian colony which existed at Bodega from 1812–1842. Leaves opposite; both disk- and ray-flowers yellow.

Seacoast Gold Fields, fig. 135

B. macrántha (large-flowered).

This, the only perennial, has the largest flower-heads in the genus. Stems 1/2–1½ ft. tall; leaves 1–3 in. long; flower-heads 3/4–1¼ in. wide. Ocean bluffs, Sonoma and Marin Cos., perhaps also San Mateo Co.: Cst. Str., Cst. Scr. Mch.–Aug.

Common Gold Fields or Sunshine, pl. 3g

B. chrysóstoma (golden mouth, for the disk-flowers).

This is the most ubiquitous species of *Baeria;* it is found from coastal dunes to inland valleys and blooms from January to May. Annual, the stems 1–10 in. tall, simple or branched; leaves linear, 1/2–1½ in. long, very

[169]

narrow or to 1/4 in. wide. Open grassy areas: Cst. Str., Cst. Scr., Oak Wood., Grass.

Two more annual Baerias are: *B. fremóntii*, its leaves with linear lobes, from e. edge of our area, and *B. mìnor* [*B. ulíginosa*], its softly woolly leaves strap-shaped with small lobes, in moist areas near coast. Both Mch.–Apr.

Monolopia, pl. 8g

Monolòpia màjor (Mono-lopia, one and husk, the single row of involucral bracts fused to form a cup around the flower-head; *major,* larger—than other Monolopias).

White-woolly annual 4–20 in. tall; leaves alternate, mostly entire; heads 1–1½ in. wide, both ray- and disk-flowers yellow. Open grassy hills or rocky slopes (in Mt. Hamilton Range often abundant in isolated colonies): Chap., Grass. Feb.–May.

× 1/2

Fig. 135

× 1/2

Fig. 136

Woolly Sunflower, fig. 136

Eriophýllum lanàtum (*Erio-phyllum*, wool and leaf, for the woolly foliage; *lanatum*, woolly).

The densely woolly foliage of young plants is responsible not only for the common name but for both parts of the scientific name. Actually, however, much of the wool may be lost with age. Perennial from a woody base, stem erect or spreading, 8–24 in. tall; leaves alternate, the upper surface green and scarcely woolly when mature; heads 3/4–1¼ in. wide, golden-yellow, single at ends of branches. Two varieties occur in our area: var. *achilleaeoìdes* of dry hills inland (Pon. Pine For., Oak Wood., Chap.) and var. *arachnoìdeum* (figured) of wooded hills near coast (Redw.–Doug. Fir. For., Bd. Ev. For., etc.), May–July.

Two other Eriophyllums, both somewhat shrubby at base and mostly summer-blooming, deserve mention because of their magnificent masses of golden-yellow flowers: Golden Yarrow (*E. confertiflòrum*) occurs in rounded bushes 1–2 ft. tall on dry rocky or brushy slopes, while Seaside Woolly Sunflower (*E. staechadifòlium*) occurs in low mats on maritime headlands. Both may open a few flowers by March. Mostly May–Nov.

Blennosperma, fig. 137

Blennosperma nànum (*Blenno-sperma*, mucous and seed, for the mucilaginous fruits; *nanum*, small) [*B. califórnicum*].

This uncommon little annual grows in very widely scattered colonies in moist open areas, as in Marin Co. where it grows only near McClure Beach (var. *robùstum*) and in Lucas Valley. Stems 4–8 in. tall, each branch ending in a flower-head; bracts of involucre in 1 row, fused at base, their tips brownish; ray-flowers cream-yellow, purplish beneath; disk-flowers cream-yellow. Oak Wood., Grass. Feb.–May.

[171]

Chaenactis, fig. 138

Chaenáctis tanacetifòlia (Chaen-actis, gape and ray, for
the ray-like disk-flowers; *tanaceti-folia,* tansy-leaved)
|*C. glabriúscula* vars. *gracilénta* and *heterocárpha* |.

Sturdy annuals 1/2–1 ft. tall, each branch ending in
a head of golden-yellow disk-flowers; ray-flowers lacking; outer row of disk-flowers much larger than inner
ones. Rocky slopes, e. side Santa Cruz Mts. and in Mt.
Hamilton Range: Oak Wood., Chap. Apr.–June.

Common Yarrow or Milfoil, fig. 139

Achillèa millefòlium (Achillea, for Achilles, first to use
it medicinally; *mille-folium,* thousand-leaved, for the
fern-like leaves) [*A. boreàlis; A. lanulòsa*].

This circumpolar Northern Hemisphere species has
been used since ancient times to treat colds, fevers,
and many other human ailments. Stems 1–3 ft. tall;
leaves finely dissected, softly hairy; flower-heads white,

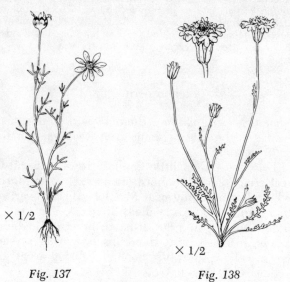

× 1/2

Fig. 137

× 1/2

Fig. 138

small, in large flat-topped clusters. From coastal bluffs to open or wooded inland slopes, sometimes weedy: many communities. Apr.–Aug.

Western Coltsfoot, fig. 140

Petasìtes palmàtus (*Peta-sites*, a broad-brimmed hat, for the huge round leaves [colt's feet]; *palmatus*, palmate, the leaves) [*P. frígidus* var. *palmatus*].

A striking but uncommon plant growing along streams in deep coastal forests. Stout perennial, the creeping rootstocks bearing erect flower-stems 6–20 in. tall and, later, long-stalked leaves with round lobed leaf-blades 5–16 in. wide and white-hairy beneath; flower-stem, with scale-like leaves, ending in a cluster of small flower-heads, these with white disk-flowers and pinkish ray-flowers. The foliage and young flower-

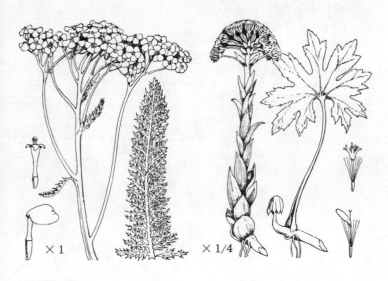

×1   ×1/4

Fig. 139   Fig. 140

[173]

heads make a good potherb, while a related European species was long used in cough remedies. Riparian Wood. in Redw.-Doug. Fir For. Mch.–June.

California Butterweed or Groundsel, fig. 141

Senècio aronicoìdes (Senecio, old man, refers to the crown of soft white hairs on each fruit; *aronic-oides,* like *Arónicum,* another sunflower).

The golden-yellow flower-heads give the name Butterweed, while Groundsel is an old folk name based on medicinal uses. Roots fibrous; stems 2–3 ft. tall; leaves woolly when young; heads 1/4–3/8 in. high, of disk-flowers only. Moist brushy or wooded slopes: Bd. Ev. For., Oak Wood., Chap. Apr.–June.

Senecio eurycéphalus [*S. bréweri*], leaves deeply divided and heads with both disk-flowers and 7–12 ray-flowers, occurs in the inner Coast Ranges. May–June.

× 1/1·2

Fig. 141

[174]

Coast Arnica, fig. 142

Árnica discoìdea (*Arnica*, lamb's skin, for the leaf texture; *discoidea,* the heads with disk-flowers only).

Arnica, well-known medicinally as tincture of arnica, is a genus of aromatically glandular, perennial herbs with opposite leaves. This species has stems 1½–2½ ft. tall; leaves coarsely toothed, to 4 in. long; heads yellow, 1/2–3/4 in. high. Open woods: Pon. Pine For., Bd. Ev. For., Chap., etc. May–July.

Thistle   *Círsium*

Cirsium, swollen vein, refers to the medicinal value reputed in early times for these prickly biennial or perennial herbs. With spines removed, the tender young stems and leaves were used by Europeans and early American settlers as a potherb. Hummingbirds act as

× 1/10

Fig. 142

pollinators of the long slender flowers of the flower-head. Leaves alternate; heads with disk-flowers only, ray-flowers absent; fruits with a ring of pappus hairs at top.

Brownie Thistle, fig. 143

C. quercetòrum (of the oak groves).

Brownie Thistle is a dwarf with usually very short stems, its flower-head clustering on the ground in the center of a leaf-circle a foot or so wide to make a spiny nosegay, or occas. its stems 4–12 in. tall. Heads 1–2 in. high; flowers purplish to white. Coastal bluffs and hills: Cst. Scr., Grass. Apr.–June.

Cobweb Thistle, pl. 8h

C. occidentàle (of the west) [*C. cóulteri*].

The flower-heads of this 1½–2 ft. tall thistle are beautifully cobwebby when young. Heads 1½–2 in.

× 1/8

Fig. 143

high; flowers crimson to purplish. Coastal sand-dunes
to inland hills: many communities. Apr.–June.

Red Thistle, fig. 144

C. proteànum (protean—exceedingly variable).
[*C. occidentàle* var. *venùstum; C. coùlteri* var. *v.*]
Plant erect, 1–5 ft. tall, less cobwebby than preceding
and flowers usually crimson but varying to purplish,
rose, or even white. Open dry slopes inland: Pon. Pine
For., Oak Wood., etc. May–Sept.

Some of the less conspicuous Bay Region spring wildflowers
of the Sunflower Family are: *Chaètopappa éxilis* [*Pentachaèta
éxilis*], slender erect annuals of open grassland, with disk- and
ray-flowers rose, the rays few, small, Apr.–May; Cottonweed
(*Micropus califórnicus*), slender, erect, white-woolly annuals of
dry open areas, with small flower-heads embedded in wool,
Mch.–May; *Psilocárphus tenéllus,* small annuals forming dense
flat mats in dry open areas, the flower-heads small, numerous,
embedded in wool. Mch.–May; *Rigiopáppus leptócladus,* small,

× 1/2

Fig. 144

erect, wiry annuals of open rocky soil, the slender branches each with a small head of yellow disk- and ray-flowers, the rays few, small, Apr.–June. Two well-established nonnative sunflowers are the large yellow-flowered Corn Chrysanthemum *(Chrysánthemum ségetum)*, a garden-escape of coastal areas mainly n. of S. F. Bay, and Brass Buttons *(Cótula coronopifólia)*, a weed from South Africa now found in our marshy coastal areas, the round flat heads of disk-flowers looking like so many yellow buttons.

SUGGESTIONS

INFORMATION AND PAMPHLETS AVAILABLE

California Conservation Council, 912 Santa Barbara St., Santa Barbara. Leaflet No. C–596 on "Wild Flowers of California; Suggestions for Conserving Them."

Office of Legislative Council, State of California, 3021 State Capitol, Sacramento. Teachers, scout leaders, etc. may write for data on California laws governing picking or removal of wildflowers or other native plants.

Public Service Office, Agricultural Extension Service, 229 University Hall, Univ. of Calif., Berkeley. Write for a list of "California Horticulturists featuring Native Plants" and for mimeographed brochures on "The Selection and Preparation of Flowering Plant Specimens" and "An Annotated Reference List to the Native Plants, Weeds, and some of the Ornamental Plants of California."

Save-the-Redwoods League, 114 Sansome St., San Francisco. Pamphlet on "Trees, Shrubs and Flowers of the Redwood Region."

Superintendent of Documents, U. S. Government Printing Office, Washington, D.C. U.S.D.A. Leaflet No. 439, "Spring-flowering Bulbs." U.S.D.A. Farmer's Bull. No. 1171, "Growing Annual Flowering Plants." Culture methods are generally appropriate to our bulb-producing and annual wildflowers.

Botanic Gardens of Bay Region Featuring Living Native Plants

Botanic Garden of East Bay Regional Parks District, Tilden Park, Berkeley. Twenty acres of California native flora in natural geographic associations, mostly woody plants.

Strybing Arboretum, Golden Gate Park, San Francisco. The Redwood Trail, southwest corner of Arboretum, contains many herbaceous perennials of the Redwood Forest. Descriptive pamphlet, "The Redwood Trail," at Hall of Flowers.

University of California Botanical Garden, Univ. of Calif., Berkeley. One section is devoted to California native plants. Many annuals and herbaceous perennials are represented.

REFERENCES [4]

General References

Harrington, H. D. *How to Identify Plants*. Denver, Colo.: Sage Books, 1957.

Lawrence, George H. M. *An Introduction to Plant Taxonomy*. New York: Macmillan Co., 1955.

Smith, Arthur C. *Introduction to the Natural History of the San Francisco Bay Region*. California Natural History Guides: 1. Berkeley: University of California Press, 1959.

References Useful in San Francisco Bay Region

Abrams, LeRoy. *Illustrated Flora of the Pacific States*. Stanford: Stanford University Press. Vol. 1, 1940; Vol. 2, 1944; Vol. 3, 1951; Vol. 4 with Roxana S. Ferris, 1960.

[4]Most of these references are available for browsing and/or sale at the Conservation Resource Center of the National Audubon Society, 2426 Bancroft Way, Berkeley 4, Calif. Its price list is available on request, and all proceeds are devoted to conservation.

Bowerman, Mary L. *The Flowering Plants and Ferns of Mount Diablo, California.* Berkeley: The Gillick Press, 1944.

Howell, John T. *Marin Flora, Manual of the Flowering Plants and Ferns of Marin County.* Berkeley: University of California Press, 1949.

Howell, John T., Peter H. Raven, and Peter Rubtzoff. *A Flora of San Francisco, California.* Wasmann Jour. Biol. 16(1): 1–157. San Francisco: University of San Francisco, 1958.

Howell, John T. and Charles Townsend. *Doorstep Botany in San Francisco.* Pacific Discovery 12(1): 14–26. San Francisco: California Academy of Sciences, 1959.

Jepson, Willis L. *A Manual of the Flowering Plants of California.* Berkeley: Associated Students Store, 1923–1925. Reprinted, 1963, by University of California Press.

Metcalf, Woodbridge. *Native Trees of the San Francisco Bay Region.* California Natural History Guides: 4. Berkeley: University of California Press, 1960.

Munz, Philip A. *A California Flora.* Berkeley: University of California Press, 1959.

Peñalosa, Javier. *A Flora of the Tiburon Peninsula, Marin County, California.* Wasmann Jour. Biol. 21(1): 1–74. San Francisco: University of San Francisco, 1963.

Rubtzoff, Peter. *A. Phytogeographical Analysis of the Pitkin Marsh* [Sonoma County]. Wasmann Jour. Biol. (11)2: 129–219. San Francisco: University of San Francisco, 1953.

Sharsmith, Helen K. *Flora of the Mount Hamilton Range of California.* American Midland Naturalist 34(2): 289–367. Notre Dame, Indiana: University of Notre Dame Press, 1945. Available from Johnson Reprint Corp., 111 Fifth Ave., N.Y. 3.

Thomas, John H. *Flora of the Santa Cruz Mountains of California*. Stanford: Stanford University Press, 1961.

How-to-do-it References

Condon, Geneal. *The Art of Flower Preservation*. A Sunset Book. Menlo Park: Lane Book Co., 1962.

Hull, Helen S. *Wildflowers for your Garden*. New York: M. Barrows & Co., Inc., 1952.

Lenz, Lee W. *Native Plants for California Gardens*. Claremont: Rancho Santa Ana Botanic Garden, 1956.

Squires, Mabel. *The Art of Drying Plants and Flowers*. New York: M. Barrows & Co., Inc., 1958.

Steffek, Edwin F. *Wild Flowers and How to Grow Them*. New York: Crown Publishers Inc., 1954.

Taylor, Kathryn S. and Stephen F. Hamblin. *Handbook of Wild Flower Cultivation*. New York: Macmillan Co., 1963.

Taylor, Norman. *Wildflower Gardening*. Princeton, N. J.: D. Van Nostrand, Inc., 1955.

INDEX TO SCIENTIFIC NAMES

(Synonyms are in italics, families in bold face type.)

[181]

[183]

INDEX TO COMMON NAMES

[189]